A MATTER

OF

TASTE

Doctors' Discovery

for

Permanent Weight Loss

If you as a dieter, have been on a "yo-yo" course all of your dieting life—losing some weight with one fad diet after another, only to gain it all back, then the moral of this book should be clear for you. Follow the doctor's rules for sensible eating and you too will discover in your personal life what the doctors discovered in their professional practice: the key to permanent weight loss is permanent weight control.

A MATTER

OF

TASTE

Doctors' Discovery
for
Permanent Weight Loss

John Pisacano, M.D.
and
Henry Lichter, M.D.

Fell's Books Fill Your Needs

FREDERICK FELL PUBLISHERS, INC., NEW YORK

Library of Congress Cataloging in Publication Data

Pisacano, John.
   A matter of taste.

   1.Obesity. 2.Taste. 3.Obesity in children.
4. Reducing. I. Lichter, Henry, joint author.
II. Title.
RC628.P57 1979   613.2'5   78-26573
ISBN 0-8119-0312-5

For information address:

Frederick Fell Publishers, Inc.
386 Park Avenue South
New York, New York 10016

Published simultaneously in Canada by:
Thomas Nelson & Sons, Limited
Don Mills, Ontario, Canada

MANUFACTURED IN THE UNITED STATES OF AMERICA

1 2 3 4 5 6 7 8 9 0

Acknowledgement

We wish to thank the following gentle people who contributed to the writing of our book:

Gladys Nyman, who personally worked with the families, counselling, encouraging and supplying the lozenges. She weighed the children and kept records.

Geraldine Bukas, who guided us in the development of the nutritional soundness of the basic diet.

Janet Lipshay, whose nutritional expertise tested the fourteen-day diet,

"Les Girls", our office staff who tolerated the "diet kids" weaving in and out of our regular practice with good humor.

To the families who were so kind to participate in the Long Beach Project.

And finally, to the following who contributed so much to A MATTER OF TASTE,

Dr. Edward L. Steinberg

Dr. Harold Silverman

Dr. Saul Heller

Dr. Jerome Knittle

Ms. Pat Hatry, Esq.

Mr. Dean Siegal

Contents

Introduction

"Where is the *new me* the last diet promised me?" We'll bet that you've asked yourself this question before.

We are pediatricians and have seen firsthand evidence that obese children often become obese adults. We have watched in alarm the nutritional sins of parents visited upon their children. As our concern with what our babies were being fed reached into childhood eating habits, a natural evolution involved us in the nutrition of their parents as well. "A house divided against itself cannot stand!"

This book was written to help you the parent avoid dietary mistakes in raising your children, and to retrain your own palates to appreciate the role that taste plays in helping you gain control of your weight.

You cannot go back in time and alter the childhood dietary mistakes that have placed you in your present plight. You must break the nutritional link that ties you to the past, and make sure that you don't build a similar chain of poor eating habits for your children.

In our own Long Beach Diet, we offer help in accustoming you to a new appreciation of the role of your sense of taste in guiding you to sensible eating habits. We hope our tips on diverting the food cravings to fulfill emotional deprivation through overeating can be conquered.

We embarked on an exciting scientific investigation which we call, "The Long Beach Project." We sought a way to use the firmly established craving for sweets in children already under the intoxication of sugar to help them lose weight. We used a medicated weight control aid to curb the intake of calories that accompanied the eating of outrageously oversweetened foods to which our children were addicted. Most of these foods are promoted on TV—foods which have been damned by concerned experts as counter-nutritional. And the audience to which all this is directed is our children!

The enthusiastic acceptance of the principles of taste control by children became contagious as more and more parents asked to participate in their own Long Beach Project. Examples of its success are mentioned throughout the book.*

We had for years been searching for a "better way" to help children avoid overeating, to develop eating habits that would enable them to grow to be lean, active and healthy adults. We developed a sound and original theory of infant feeding that we use to enlighten the mothers of the children we treat in our daily practice.

The major difference the Long Beach Diet offers you is TASTE, which we deliberately stress in each day's diet plan. The essential factor of our approach to the control of overeating is the satisfaction of your sense of taste first. If you do not make your food exciting to your palate, you miss the point of this book. Let us show you how!

You'll be especially interested in reading the research studies of other physicians and scientists included in this book in the area of taste control, reinforcing what the Long Beach Project showed us.

As you read this book, and practice the approach to food and dieting we suggest, take nothing on faith—

*Portions of our manuscript were published in *Pediatrics*, the official publication of the American Academy of Pediatrics, *Briefs*, the publication of the Maternity Center Association and *Human Nature* magazine.

accept only what your own experience proves to be true. Your scale and mirror will tell you the truth.

J.P.
H.L.

PREFACE

Obesity—The Lingering National Epidemic

Obesity is one of the most common diseases in the United States, affecting a significant portion of the adult population. A seemingly endless number of treatments for obesity have been tried, each offering the last word in management. They include diets, drugs, hormones, hypnosis and other types of psychotherapy as well as mechanical and electrical devices for the removal of local accumulations of fat. The continued proliferation of new methods and agents indicates the relative failure of all in promoting sustained loss of weight in most obese persons.

In this book, Drs. Pisacano and Lichter have presented a simple yet revolutionary approach to the problem of excess fat: STOP IT AT THE SOURCE. As pediatricians, they instruct their toddlers' parents how to control their children's taste. With this basic approach, a child learns to control his weight without feeling hungry. Their investigations revealed that obesity's earliest danger signals were demonstrated in infant and child feeding patterns. From this study, the obvious links between taste, appetite and obesity emerged. It became evident that the most natural way to assure a slim and correspondingly healthy adult is to structure both eating habits and food selection patterns at a very early age.

Using rules and lessons developed and conceptualized in their pediatric practice, the authors challenged deeply ingrained child-rearing food patterns. Slowly and cauti-

15

ously they had to re-educate parents in the revolutionary new concept of "taste control" as the key to "appetite control."

The authors were aware of and concerned with the revealing statistics that have emerged from the Korean War and Vietnam War which showed an alarming incidence of advanced arteriosclerosis in apparently healthy young American casualties. Research into younger age groups indicated that cardiovascular problems actually exist in youngsters, even beginning with three-year-olds. Arteriosclerosis, or "hardening of the arteries," which in its early stages is called atherosclerosis is one of the chief causes of death in the United States.

The first evidence of atherosclerosis is the fatty streak. Fatty streaking is a medical term for the accumulation in the walls of arteries of fatty substances called lipids. By the age of ten, fatty streaks are present in the aorta of every child, regardless of race, sex or environment. Fatty streaks are related to excessively high concentrations of lipids or fat-related substances in the blood—a condition called hyperlipidemia which can eventually lead to atherosclerosis, heart disease, heart attacks and stroke.

Although the mystery of why cholesterol and other lipids are deposited and harden in the arterial walls of man remains unsolved, the available evidence indicates that diets high in both saturated fat (animal fats and saturated vegetable oils) and highly refined carbohydrate (sugar) lead to hyperlipidemia, while diets low in these substances but higher in unsaturated fats (non-hydrogenated vegetable fats and polyunsaturated oils) do not. It is an obvious conclusion that proper dietary habits instilled at an early age can minimize the chances of obesity and prevent attendant problems later in life.

The question the authors faced was how to teach proper dieting and have their patients maintain good dietary habits throughout their lives. Research into the role of taste in appetite and weight control in animals supported the authors' belief that to correct the problems of obesity, one should start with the child and the food that he eats. Obesity and its accompanying problems need not be thrust upon the unsuspecting child by well-intentioned parents. By re-educating parents in the basics of good nutrition, it seemed possible to condition their children's palates to acquire tastes for the correct foods which would carry them all through life. The authors have succeeded in making their approach to diet an exciting human experience.

You will want to read this fascinating book both for sheer enjoyment and its important message regarding dietary re-education. Overtaste, the enemy within, can be overcome at an early age.

H. I. Silverman, D.Sc.
Associate Dean,
Professor of Pharmacy and Director
Division of Applied Sciences, Massachusetts College of Pharmacy
Lecturer in Community Medicine, Boston University School of Medicine

FOREWORD

Basic Facts On Obesity

> "Persons who are very fat are apt to die earlier than those who are slender."
>
> Hippocrates (460-377 B.C.)

For over two thousand years medical science has known that obesity is a condition in which the amount of fat stored in the body is excessive, resulting in a general or local accumulation of fat tissue and undesirable increase in body weight that may shorten one's life.

People do not realize this simple fact of life: obesity is not only an aesthetic problem but a serious medical problem. The excess fat invades inner organs and impairs their function.

Obesity has three deleterious effects:

1. It impairs one aesthetically.
2. It undermines one's health and shortens one's life.
3. It harms one emotionally and mentally.

When one is obese, the vital organs are overloaded. Although the normal human body is a nearly perfect machine, in the obese individual, the heart and the lungs have no choice but to overwork. The pulse is rapid, the blood pressure rises, there is difficulty in breathing, and swelling of the ankles is common. In such a condition, overexertion is a danger of life and health.

There are about 70,000,000 overweight people in the United States. Excess calories is the basic cause! When the calorie intake of food exceeds the caloric expenditure in the form of work and heat, the excess is converted into fat and stored in the body. Thus, too much food of any kind is fattening. (In this connection it should be mentioned that alcohol is a concentrated food of high caloric value.)

It must always be borne in mind that overweight is due to an oversupply of food calories. Voracious appetites are the most common cause of excessive caloric intake.

Nervous states often stimulate the appetite and cause excessive intake. This will result in obesity. Many people who enjoy food more than others eat more than they require and become fat.

A lower base metabolic rate, which is usually due to glandular deficiencies, will lead to obesity if one's food intake is maintained at the level of the average normal person. However, low metabolic rates account for only a very small percentage of obesity, whereas most overweight people have normal base metabolic rates.

Many women show extreme gain in weight after the menopause. This is caused primarily by increased food intake or decrease in physical activity, or both. Unfortunately, the obesity in these women often develops as local fat deposits.

The intake of food in many people is balanced with their caloric requirements, without conscious regulation of their food intake. Here, the metabolism of the body is in harmony with the psychological drives which govern appetite, the fullness of the stomach and the degree of both physical and mental activity.

When pleasure in eating becomes a dominant, overwhelming personality trait, the senses of fullness and satisfaction after a meal may require an excessive intake of food. This leads to addiction to food, which stifles ambition, curtails inter-personal relationships and results in obesity. In such cases obesity is a symptom of emotional maladjustment.

Both psychological factors and physiological factors are usually the specific causes of obesity and therefore both of these factors must be evaluated in the obese.

Obesity causes shortness of breath and fatigue and places abnormal stress upon the knee joints and the lower back, where arthritis is prone to develop. The increased strain on the heart circulation and respiration causes hypertension in the young and old.

Proper eating habits of those predisposed to obesity must be established and appropriate physical activity must become a daily habit. Since the immediate cause of obesity is always a caloric intake in excess of the daily requirements, a lowering of food intake is always necessary to produce weight loss. The protein allowance should be liberal while carbohydrates should be chosen primarily from low-carbohydrate fruits and vegetables. The fat intake should be minimal. The diet should be adequate in calcium, iron and vitamins, and when necessary, it should be supplemented with vitamin concentrates. Restriction of salt is advisable for those who tend to retain fluid.

Advice from a sympathetic physician is always helpful. However, the mere prescription of a diet is not enough. In many cases, due to the fact that the taste of food has become an overwhelming personality trait, it is difficult to follow a prescribed diet. This is quite prevalent in both adults and children. In this large group, certain safe medications which decrease and tame the appetite help achieve weight loss, as indicated by some of the interesting case histories in this book.

A simple, safe preparation that is not stimulating or habit forming and one that can be used by both adults and children is most desirable. The use of such a preparation can lead to weight loss in obesity by decreasing the appetite, thus helping to normalize food intake.

Americans must learn to prevent obesity as well as to control it, to maintain normal weight levels as well as to regain them. It is for this reason that the treatment of obesity has become so important a part of pediatric practice and that the prevention of obesity is now becoming part of what pediatricians call "well baby care," as the authors of this book have so clearly indicated.

Saul I. Heller, M.D.

Life Fellow, American Psychiatric Association
Member, American Academy of Neurology
Diplomate in Psychiatry and Neurology
American Board of Psychiatry and Neurology
Past President, New York State Board of Medicine

Section I

TASTE CONTROL

CHAPTER 1

Taste and Your Appetite

Into our office over the past twenty-two years of pediatric practice have come thousands of parents with fat children. Very often the parents are fat too.

Whenever we see that, we worry because there is an 80 percent chance that fat children will become fat grown-ups. Fat people have shorter, sicker lives than people who are not fat.

We are doctors and we are fathers. Between us, we have eight children of our own. We want all the children we take care of to live long, healthy lives, which means we do not want them to be fat.

"Why are we fat, Doctor?" a mother asks.

"Because you and your family eat too much," we answer.

"But why do we eat too much?"

"To get extra pleasure through taste."

A pause. A moment of thought.

Most of our overweight patients had never thought about taste before. Had you?

"Okay, Doctor," the mother says, "but why do we want extra pleasure through taste?"

"Because when you were a child," we answer, "you were fed in such a way that you developed the habit of overeating, and with it, the habit of overtasting. This habit is not just in your head. It is in your cells which developed an extra capacity for holding fat by the time

25

you were a teenager. And it is in your taste patterns. The foods you learned to love when you were young have captured your sense of taste. They may have been the most fattening, unhealthful foods around. If you want to lose weight now, you will have to re-train your sense of taste to make it respond to different, less fattening foods!"

Psychologically Speaking

Most physicians agree that the vast majority of obese individuals suffer from simple overeating beyond the needs of the body and the energy expenditure. For years, researchers in the field have felt emotional factors form a large part of the obese person's problem and contribute to eating disorders.

Freud spoke of the developmental phases each child goes through, called psychosexual stages. He was referring to particular sources of pleasure which become increasingly important during early childhood development.

Dr. S.R. Bortner, a psychiatrist at Saint Vincent's Hospital in New York, reminds us that the first stage, the oral phase, is for many the most significant. It is during this time of life that specific personality patterns may surface which influence later development. During this phase, the child relates to his world through his mouth. Most of his sources of pleasure are related to oral gratification, for example, hunger, thumbsucking, teething, eating.

Factors other than those which fulfill the body's needs soon enter the picture and behavioral patterns are born. A youngster soon learns to evoke the approval or anger of his parents by accepting or rejecting foods. Specific tastes become associated with pleasurable parent/child interaction; denial of these tastes, with friction and unpleasantness. These patterns develop early in life and become a part of adult behavior.

The obese adult often eats to pacify some inner need or to help him through times of stress. It's not the full, bloated sensation he craves, but the fantasy of specific foods; he visualizes, feels, smells and tastes the desired food. He learned at a very young age that specific foods and/or tastes are associated with pleasure and reward, and the person eats them in an attempt to recapture the pleasant experience.

Figure 1 shows the never ending cycle of the overeater. His craving for specific foods resulting in overeating and weight gain produces only dissatisfaction with himself and unpleasant feelings, only to attempt to recapture the pleasant ones by overeating. Dr. Bortner suggests that the best time to break this cycle is at the point of taste craving. By reducing the taste sensation, the food craving reward segment can be dramatically altered. If it is applied repeatedly, the eradication of this sector is gradually reinforced. Once the cycle is interrupted with regularity and in conjunction with a supervised nutritional program, weight loss becomes the reward and replaces the food craving as a reward.

Your "Pleasure Economy": Overeating Is A Poor Investment

Whatever you have been doing to lose weight, it will help you immeasurably to understand this basic fact about your appetite.

Each of us has his own special "Pleasure Economy." We want as much pleasure from life as we can get. That is natural. On the other hand, no one is lucky enough to live in a state of pure pleasure: we lose our jobs, we get strapped for money, our children get into trouble, our

FIGURE 1

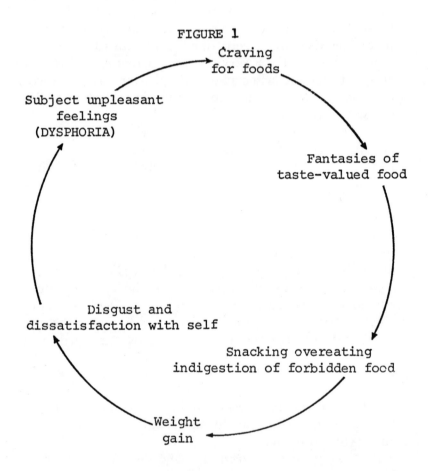

Craving
for foods

Subject unpleasant
feelings
(DYSPHORIA)

Fantasies of
taste-valued food

Disgust and
dissatisfaction with self

Snacking overeating
indigestion of forbidden food

Weight
gain

marriages collapse, or some other emotionally disastrous situation. There are just some days when we "should have stood in bed," when we "cannot make a nickel" and our "Pleasure Economy" goes bankrupt.

Your "Pleasure Economy" is the balance you make between the *pleasure* and the *pain* that comes into your life each day. Most of what you do—certainly most of what you eat—is part of your effort to create pleasure income to pay yourself back for the various pleasure deficits you have to endure. The trouble is that, like a lot of economists, you sometimes make mistakes. You put your faith in certain pleasure incomes that do not work out. The way many people have found to bring themselves additional pleasure income is to eat, to get some extra pleasure through taste. If some eating brings you some pleasure income, you may grow to believe that a lot of eating will bring you a lot of pleasure income. That is where your theory of nutritional economics goes wrong. Overeating is a bad investment.

How do you discover that overeating is a bad investment to make in your "Pleasure Economy"? When you find that you are on your way to becoming sick or unattractive.

There has to be a better way to find this out. We tell all our patients to think for a moment about their sense of taste.

"Compensatory Overtasting": Is the Rich Reward Worth the Risk?

Food is a dependable source of pleasure. You have known that from the day you were born, and were cuddled up to a breast or a bottle. You can count on food. At the very least it will fill your stomach. With a little effort at preparation and selection, you can make any food perfectly satisfying.

Now eating is fun, but *overeating* is harmful. Just as tasting is fun, *overtasting* can ruin your health.

Take the case of Dorothy N.:

When Dorothy was a little girl, her father died and her mother disappeared. She was brought up by her mother's parents who loved her dearly. They did everything they could to make her happy. One of the things they did was to overfeed her with all the wrong kinds of foods: cake and ice cream and mashed potatoes and sauerbraten with gravy, a specialty of their German-American home. Dorothy got used to the taste of those foods and learned to associate them with love. Her eating habits and her taste patterns as well were formed back in those days.

When Dorothy came home from church on Sundays, her grandmother would give her some money to go out and buy a strawberry shortcake. The little girl would run happily off to the baker and return home with a big strawberry shortcake that her grandmother would then cut exactly in half. One half would be divided between grandmother, grandfather and her uncle. The other half—all of it—would be gobbled up by little Dorothy.

Why was she not satisfied with a normal-sized piece of cake? Why did she have to eat the entire half?

The answer is that she did not have to eat the entire half. If left alone, her "Pleasure Economy" would have been satisfied by an average-sized serving. However, her grandmother was using the strawberry shortcake probably as the only way she knew how to say "We are sorry your mother left you" and "This huge piece of sweet, cream-filled cake is our way of trying to make up for your loss."

From Dorothy's point of view, she assumed that her grandmother was trying to teach her something. She figured that if she ate the average-sized piece of cake, it would taste good and give her a certain amount of pleasure. At the same time she was being taught that an even larger piece would give her even more taste pleasure.

Of course, she was wrong. (No child can be expected to be a good personal pleasure economist. See Rules for Enlightened Feeding.) It was in Dorothy's little head that the idea of more-is-better got started. She thought it was so terrific to receive extra pleasure income through taste that she was learning to ignore the signals her stomach was sending her: that after an average-sized serving, she was really full.

This is what we call "Compensatory Overeating." Dorothy was being taught to make her sense of taste pay her back for the loss of pleasure elsewhere. (It is pretty *clear* where the loss was; no matter how loving her grandparents were, it was hard not to feel like a deserted child when that is exactly what she was.)

Even though Dorothy's case is extreme, the principles still hold. And if you are overweight, most likely "Compensatory Overtasting" is what you are doing, too. Long after the pleasure deficit is gone, you continue to overtaste because it is a habit. Your palate demands it. Your metabolism demands it. Your psyche demands it. It has also become a habit to ignore the "full" signals that your satisfied stomach naturally tries to send you.

If Dorothy N. could somehow feel that she had compensated herself for her pleasure deficit with just a moderate amount of food, then she would not have been a fat child and she would not have grown into an obese woman who weighed over 200 pounds in her early twenties. The trouble was, she ate too much (she was fed too much), in order to right the balance.

It is a logical conclusion, then, that the secret of successful dieting is to train yourself to get the same amount of taste pleasure from a smaller amount of food, and at the same time, from less fattening foods.

How Many Warnings Do We Need Before the Heart Attack?

Most people know how dangerous it is to be over-weight. We doctors are the voices of doom when it comes to obesity, and now the United States government and insurance companies have joined the chorus. But children do not listen to such voices. While their mothers are bringing them up on pizza, frosty freeze and french fries, the children are not worrying about diabetes, heart disease or hypertension. They do not know of such things. They are just happy to gobble up the goodies. (We call them "baddies.")

Only their mothers can listen to the warnings—and understand them.

But what happens if the mothers do not listen? Too many children *may* grow up with a tendency toward diabetes, heart disease, hypertension or strokes. And of course, just as with smoking, mothers and fathers go right on overfeeding themselves and their children, ignoring the frightening warnings of the experts.

When Dorothy N. (the strawberry shortcake girl) grew up, she was very fat. So was her young uncle who lived with her as a child.

"He started eating when I was in high school," she recalls, "eating and eating; more and more. He married a fat woman and they overate together. Finally, he got sick and was hospitalized. He was put on a very strict diet, but his wife would smuggle food in to him: hamburgers; not just one, but something like a pound of chopped meat dripping with grease on a big roll. He would have three or four smuggled in at one time and eat all of them. And my grandfather would say to me, 'Your uncle is going to kill himself with eating. You watch!' "

Grandpa was right: Dorothy's uncle died of a stroke before he was fifty.

For Dorothy N., his death was the warning that finally worked. She had been tuning out the advice of doctors for years. Then, through the simple, slow, sure method of taste control she lost 85 pounds and became a slim, healthy person for the first time in her life. Learn to control your sense of taste!

We must learn to distinguish hunger from appetite. Hunger is that instinct which signals the body's need for food. Newborn children experience hunger, not appetite. Appetite, on the other hand, is based on those memories of past eating pleasures (like those Dorothy N. so often remembered) that determine food likes and dislikes.

Listen to the warnings of knowledgeable people who are informed and concerned. Do not wait for a death in the family. The death, after all, might be your own.

A Successful Dieter Is A Hero: The Odds Are Against You

Even if you take into consideration the grim prospects for overweight Americans, it is difficult to find the willpower to diet. If you have found this to be your trouble, do not blame yourself entirely. You have some powerful enemies who got together to keep you fat.

First, there is the multi-million-dollar food industry, constantly producing new "baddies" to tempt you.

Second, there is the multi-million-dollar packaging industry, presenting everything so it looks like it is going to taste terrific. You would practically have to be tasteless not to respond.

Third, is the multi-million-dollar food advertising industry —unless it is selling diet or low-calorie

33

products—whose purpose it is to make you buy more and eat more. (There is one clever advertising jingle that tries to sell you the idea of having "more than one." It never seems to occur to the food industry that one is probably enough.)

The fact of the matter is, hundreds of thousands of people are making their living by keeping you fat.

You also have enemies within.

Subtle, devious little demons operate in silence, so automatically deep within your subconscious that you hardly notice them. They are the demands of your body, the demands of your psyche, the demands of the pleasure economy that took hold of your life when you were most vulnerable—when you were young.

How many times have we heard mothers say they reward their children with chocolate?

"Take your bath, brush your teeth, snuggle in bed and don't give me any trouble, and I'll give you a piece of chocolate."

Some mothers have been known to say that. Did yours? Or worse, "Eat all your string beans and I'll give you some ice cream." If you have ever been a parent who made statements like these, then you know who your child's enemy is. As Walt Kelly's cartoon character Pogo said, "We have met the enemy and he is us!"

Sweets are not a reward! They are a national curse! If a mother rewards a child with sweets from the time he is an infant, it is going to be extremely difficult to get him to cut down on sweets when he is an overweight seven year old. It is going to be even harder when the child is thirty or forty. To reward a child with fattening food is a way of training his sense of taste to desire the wrong foods forever.

Guideline number one: A child's taste for sweets must be curbed—not encouraged!

Well then, what about those of us who are already fat, whose mothers thought fat babies were cute, and pudgy toddlers were charming? Obviously, we have to do something about it; we cannot just let a badly-trained sense of taste ruin our lives. *We have to diet, to change our eating habits, to retrain our sense of taste.* This means a big change in your habitual pleasure economy, which is not an easy accomplishment.

In short, when you start a serious reducing diet, you are attempting an heroic confrontation. You are entitled to all the help you can get.

Tell The Whole World That You're Dieting

Few people lose weight until they find the inner motivation to do so. Motivation comes in strange ways, different for every individual, depending on his or her age and stage. This is discussed in greater detail in "The Ages of Overtaste."

Once you acquire a reason to be slim, beautiful and healthy (inner motivation), success in dieting depends on three things: whether you can continue wanting to be slim, beautiful and healthy (this is really the easy part); what point of entry you choose for your diet (this *is* the hard part); and, what you use to help you stay on your diet (it will be easier if you learn to believe in taste control).

Dieting is not just a game. It is a deadly serious duel to the finish between your old mis-trained sense of taste and your new-found inner motivation. Your goal is to train yourself to stop your bad eating habits and replace them with good eating habits. If you are victorious, you succeed in acquiring a whole new pleasure economy.

The point of entry is crucial. It is like stepping onto a

35

whirling merry-go-round or under a snapping jump rope. Choose the wrong time to get into the process and you will probably have to start over.

Why do you think the various diet clubs have met with so much success? When a point of entry is observed by other people, you are much more likely to stay in the process. It is very hard to go back on a commitment you have made before an audience.

In Long Beach, the suburban New York town where we practice medicine, an experimental diet program has been put into practice in two public schools. Children who are overweight share their problems and their difficulties with dieting. They work together at it, committing themselves to one another. In this program the point of entry into the diet is observed by other people and supervised by other people. In addition, it occurs in the elementary school years when it is easier for both the body and the psyche to tackle the process of taking off weight.

Guideline number two: Give yourself an honest break; do not begin a diet in secret.

To Diet Is Not To Suffer!

Why do so many people expect dieting to make them suffer? They have been brought up on what we call "Negative Dieting." Do not eat this, do not eat a lot of that, do not, do not, do not.

Such people choose only those diets that force them to go through horrible deprivation, dreadful hunger and the agonizing loss of beloved tastes.

No sugar. "Not ever!" one diet says. And so you live without sugar, without the taste of real sweetness on your tongue.

You start yelling at your children and snarling at your

spouse. The sight of a six-year-old with an ice cream cone can make you tremble with temptation; the thought of a cake somewhere in the house can make you breathless with longing.

No diet can do its job—which is to help you lose weight—if it makes you suffer. No human being who feels miserable, uptight, deprived and worthless, can possibly expect to stay in a process that is as long and subtle as a proper diet. We would rather see you get into the habit of "positive dieting"—do eat fish, do eat salad, do eat fresh fruit.

In fact, dieting should eliminate nothing but excess!

Diets that shove people into one or another nutritional corner are temporary agonies. There you are, struggling to limit your intake of food, on a fad diet that simply substitutes one excess for another.

As soon as people resume their normal eating habits, they invariably gain back all the weight they lost while they were "cornered."

"I was on the grapefruit diet," Dorothy N. recalled.

"How did that work?" we asked.

"I was so sick of grapefruit that I got nauseous at the sight of one."

The same thing is true of any "fad food" diet. We absolutely believe that any diet which a well person tries must include a variety of tastes. Dorothy N., with her "mashed potato hangup," once tried to quell her desire for the taste of mashed potatoes by eating candy instead. She stayed just as fat on the candy, got bored with its taste and only aggravated her desire for mashed potatoes.

Any diet that severely limits the variety of tastes and textures that may cross your palate is bound to fail in the long run. The long run is very important: the long run is your life.

The diet that will really work for you is the diet that will provide you with a new way of eating to last for years and years to come. Therefore, the diet you go on now should introduce you to a way of eating that will last the rest of your life.

The worst fad diet, in our estimation, was a medical fad—the amphetamine-aided diet. Amphetamines were those little "uppers" that the doctors of some dieters dispensed. We had patients whose college-age brothers and sisters took amphetamines to stay awake in order to study the whole night before a test. These pills made them nervous and jumpy; sometimes they caused a good mood and other times they resulted in a bad mood. But because they were habit-forming stimulants, they altered the mood.

When the effect of the amphetamines wore off, the students were starving and exhausted. So, in order to keep their appetites under control, they had to take another amphetamine. And another. Our Dorothy N. tried these, too. She became, in her own words, "an amphetamine junkie," and naturally, it ruined her health and resulted in her hospitalization. Luckily for her, a sensible physician intervened and helped her go "cold turkey."

It is fortunate for all of you, the government intervened and limited the prescribing of amphetamines for dieters. Some states have even eliminated them as a tool for weight control. Physicians who prescribe them in these states risk losing their licenses!

As long as you expect dieting to be a miserable interlude, it must fail! Here is guideline three: Get used to the idea of "Positive Dieting." Nutritious food can be tasty and low calorie!

If you weigh too much, then the gap between sensible eating and the way you eat is the area of excess—the area that is making you fat. It is in that crucial area that you are indulging in compensatory overtasting, seeking too much pleasure from the taste of food and ignoring the signals from your stomach that you are full.

What is sensible eating?

We suggest the Long Beach Diet modified by us in our own practice for our young patients. We advise parents to follow this diet for their children and themselves (not just the overweight children) from the time those youngsters are eight months old. The Long Beach Diet is a prime example of positive dieting. Every kind of good taste is included in it but there is no room for overtaste. If you follow these guidelines, your market basket will be just as full, probably a lot greener, and surely a lot less weighted down with fat, just as you will be.

This was the kind of dieting that transformed Dorothy N. from a 185-pound individual to a gorgeous woman wearing a size seven dress.

"To help me stay within the guidelines of my diet," she recalled, "I used a special medicated gum for weight control.* I found that if I chewed the gum and drank a glass of water before meals, and between meals when I was hungry, my sense of taste was curbed and I could control my appetite."

The longer she stayed on the Long Beach Diet, the closer Dorothy N. came to re-training her mis-directed sense of taste that had been created in childhood and

---

*The gum used by Dorothy N. was Slim-Mint Gum, a product of the Thompson Medical Company, New York, N.Y.

which had made her into an obese woman. As her sense of taste was retrained, Dorothy N. found it easier and easier to resist the temptation of foods that had made her fat. She learned to like her new foods as much as she had liked her old foods. In other words, she had learned the technique of positive dieting.

Guideline number four: Sensible eating is positive dieting, dieting you like, dieting you can live with forever, dieting that satisfies your sense of taste and brings it under control at the same time.

CHAPTER 2

What Is Taste Control?

When we are very hungry, before a late afternoon Thanksgiving dinner for example, we are glad to taste the celery and olives and the cheese and crackers the hostess serves as an appetizer. Then comes the turkey and dressing, which everyone gobbles up with a zest that begins to wear thin as we reach for second helpings. We then wonder why the appetizer tasted so good when, by this time, the turkey has lost its appeal.

Just when we think we cannot eat another thing, the hostess brings out her freshly baked pumpkin pie. Of course, everyone finds room for a piece. The moral of this holiday example is: as we become full, food tends to lose its pleasurability for us, and we attempt to recapture that initial pleasure.

Perhaps this is why desserts are served at the end of meals—to prolong the pleasure gained from food sensations despite the full feeling that turns these pleasures off. By pursuing these pleasures, we remedy our food needs, until the need arises again and the pleasurability of taste reappears. This is the way we stay regulated as to body weight and dietary balance.

Some people experience too much pleasure from certain dimensions of taste such as sweetness. The temptations of food, the sight, smell and taste are too much to resist. The result for many is obesity, and researchers have looked to decrease hunger in ways other than feeding.

At the University of Pennsylvania, a group of scientists under the leadership of Dr. Philip Teitelbaum launched a series of laboratory experiments to determine how taste really works. His research team investigated taste, appetite, motivation, hunger, and their effects on food intake and obesity in laboratory animals.

We realize the incomparable differences between the brain of a rat and that of a man, but we also know that similar cells of all animals work in essentially the same way. We studied Dr. Teitelbaum's conclusions and wondered if they could be applied to our concepts of the role that taste plays in eating.

Dr. Teitelbaum and his research team had developed a way of feeding animals directly into the stomach totally bypassing and leaving out of the eating process the area of taste perception in the mouth and the sense of smell in the nose.

What happened?

When the normal rat was deprived of taste it fed itself only when hunger pangs triggered the animal's need for food, without the influence of taste maintaining normal food intake and weight.

As Dr. Teitelbaum and his colleagues concluded, ". . . Oropharangeal sensations determine the rate and duration of the overeating and are essential for maximum levels of obesity."*

Laboratory evidence has shown that when the lateral hypothalamus, located at the center of the brain, is electrically stimulated, a rat will eat and keep on eating until the stimulus stops.

*Dennis McGinty, Alan Epstein and Philip Teitelbaum, "The Contribution of Oropharyngeal Sensations to Hypothalmic Hyperphagia." *Animal Behavior,* 13, IV, October 1965.

In the research laboratories of a leading New York university, Dr. Edgar Coons experimented with rats who were given as much food as they wanted until they could eat no more. These same rats were then electrically stimulated through a probe inserted into their brains. The researchers then took a base reading to determine how much electrical stimulus was required to make the satiated rat eat even more.*

Later on, sense of taste of the rats was reduced by applying a mild, topical anesthetic on their tongues. The rats were again electrically stimulated and offered an unlimited quantity of food. The researchers found that a higher electrical stimulus was then necessary to make the satiated rats eat when taste and oral sensations are reduced with a topical anesthetic. It was concluded that when the tongue is anesthetized and eating pleasure reduced, the amount of food eaten will be reduced.

Dr. Kurt Konigsbacher, a scientific researcher from Boston, Massachusetts, set out to measure the effectiveness of a mild, topical anesthetic in reducing the taste sensation in human subjects.

In a double blind clinical study, professional taste testers were asked to taste three different liquids, one salty, one sweet and one bitter, and rate their flavor strength on a nine-point scale ranging from "very strong" to "flavorless".

Then the taste testers were given two pieces of chewing gum, one containing a mild, topical anesthetic (benzocaine), and one piece of ordinary chewing gum, not knowing the test gum from the plain gum. Subjects were told to chew the first piece of gum to the beat of a metronome to insure a uniform number of chews, and then again rate the same solutions on the same rating scale.

*Grill, Harvey J., and Coons, Edgar E., Doctoral Dissertation, *Feeding Behavior, the CNS Weighting of Sweetness and Hunger, 1976.*

43

The following day, after chewing the second piece of gum to the beat of the metronome, the subjects rated the flavor strength of the liquids for a third time.

The ratings consistently showed a statistically significant reduction in the taste sensation for all three solutions after chewing the benzocaine gum. Plain gum did not reduce the taste sensitivity to any great degree. The conclusion was a mild, local anesthetic *was* effective in significantly reducing taste sensitivity in human subjects.

In the 1973 clinical study by Drs. McClure and Brusch,* two physicians and independent clinical researchers from Cambridge, Massachusetts, tested the effectiveness of dieting with a benzocaine lozenge against four other methods: prescription amphetamine products, Ayds candy, will power alone and a plain lozenge. The group using the benzocaine lozenge lost significantly more weight each week than any other test group and lost more weight overall for the study period.

Oral Satisfaction and Obesity

Most physiology textbooks indicate that eating is under the control of brain structures located in a region called the hypothalamus, more specifically, the lateral hypothalamus. However, new research suggests that it is also the mouth, and not only the lateral hypothalamus that turns on hunger and makes us eat or overeat.

Researchers have pointed to the trigeminal nerve network, the system that carries information about touch, temperature and pain from the mouth and face to the brain, as a major influence in appetite control. It is into a branch of the trigeminal nerve that your dentist injects

*McClure, Charles W., M.D. and Brusch, Charles A., M.D., "Treatment of Oral Syndrome Obesity with Non-Traditional Appetite Control Plan," *Journal of the American Women's Medical Association*, 28: 239-248, 1973.

Novocaine to eliminate pain during dental work.

Studies conducted by Dr. H.P. Ziegler on pigeons and rats showed that damage to the trigeminal nerve network resulted in a loss of appetite.* Damage to the lateral hypothalamus had no affect on appetite.

His research suggests that the trigeminal system is only one link in an entire feeding circuit made up of structures located at various brain levels. The oral sensa·tions that pour into this feeding circuit guide and coordinate our desire to eat, and along with taste, arouse our appetites and motivate our eating behavior. Considering the fact that the trigeminal system is sensitive to oral touch, it's easy to see that it may be the smoothness of chocolate mousse or the crispness of a cornchip that results in overeating as much as it is their sweet or salty taste, or the emptiness of the stomach.

It is said that fat people are often more sensitive to food-related stimuli. Many of these obese people eat normal meals, but continue to snack all day long. Ziegler's studies point out that it may not be hunger, but the sensation of food in the mouth that keeps them going.

In another study by R.E. Nisbett,** two groups of people, one obese, the other normal, were told that they were selected to test a delicious, new flavor of vanilla ice cream. The subjects were told to eat as much of the ice cream as they wanted. The obese group ate more of the ice cream than the normal weight group.

A week later, the same two groups of people were brought together to test the same vanilla flavor, to which quinine sulfate, a bitter substance had been added to

*Ziegler, H.P., *Psychology Today,* "The Sensual Feel of Food," August, 1975: 62-66.

**Nisbett, R.E., *Journal Pers. .Soc. Psychol.* "Taste, Deprivation and Weight Determinants of Eating Behavior." 10: 107-116, 1968.

purposely modify the good taste. The normal subjects ate about the same amount. The obese subjects again ate more of the taste-modified ice cream than the normal subjects. Although the obese subject again ate more of the taste modified ice cream, they ate less than before. In fact, the amount they consumed nearly approached the normal level.

Therefore, obese people appear to be more responsive to taste modification than normal weight people. When taste was modified, obese subjects ate an amount more nearly equal to the amount eaten by normal weight people. This is exactly our point—control your sense of taste and you'll eat less.

What Happens to the Tasteless?

What happens to people with no sense of taste?

Ask the lady who has just been to the dentist and had her mouth shot full of large doses of Novocaine. Most likely, she will not be interested in eating the minute she steps out of the chair.

Another way of being tasteless has to do with memory.

Imagine that some awful turn of fate has numbed your tongue permanently. Your taste buds are sleeping. Across your palate and all around your mouth there is a kind of numbness, like that induced by your dentist's Novocaine. You cannot taste flavor nor feel texture.

At first, you might still desire the treats like chocolate chiffon pie that are probably making you fat now. Your sense of taste, programmed through your memory, would still be triggering your appetite.

But then, after a while, you would begin to forget what chocolate chiffon pie actually tasted like. The crispy crust, the smooth cool chocolate filling, the rich thick whipped cream topping would all become distant memories for you. In fact, you would become like a little child who has never eaten a piece of chocolate chiffon pie who can easily push it away because he has no idea of how good it tastes.

As pediatricians, we see people with brand new taste buds every day. These patients are brand new people—newborn infants. Babies do not know that skim milk is not as rich and creamy as whole milk. At the babies' three-month visit, when we usually stop the formula, we tell the mothers to give them skim milk from here on. We do not offer babies whole milk because we are training those baby taste buds to love skim milk. Give that baby whole milk at age three and he will probably not like it—the texture will be too heavy and creamy for him. The same is accomplished with every other kind of rich, sweet, fatty food that does either too little or too much for children nutritionally. Thus we score another victory for weight control through taste control.

If every mother would reward her children with wonderful, delicious, crisp salad, we might just grow up a nation of slim, healthy, beautiful people.

Controlling Your Sense of Taste: Clinical Proof

Such a state of affairs is a pediatrician's dream, of course. However, we think we have found a method to help our dream of taste control come true.

In July 1958, Dr. Milton Plotz wrote a short article in the *Medical Times** reporting tests he had made on overweight patients with a special medicated gum. Dr. Plotz based his approach upon the use of benzocaine in products to reduce the desire to smoke.

*Plotz, Milton, M.D., *Medical Times.* "Obesity." 86: 860-863, 1958.

What has a cure for smoking got to do with reducing appetite? The answer is simple! Both appetite and smoking are a matter of taste.

The sales promoters of cigars and cigarettes discovered long ago that people who smoke do so to satisfy a desire for pleasure through taste. That is why cigarettes are often advertised as though they were food: Winston does not look good—it "tastes good, like a cigarette should." That is why you are asked to enjoy "the fresh taste of a Salem." Your palate is the playing field.

When you combine certain specific essential oils with benzocaine, it becomes even more effective in suppressing taste. Oil of spearmint, peppermint, cinnamon and cloves. Stop to think of it. You will realize that the flavors of these oils in their purest form are overwhelming to the taste buds . . . naturally.

Try some experiments.

Chew a peppermint, not a gentle sweet one, but a strong-smelling peppermint—the kind with the ice-cold taste. Now, right away, eat a piece of salami. Until the peppermint taste dies away, that salami will taste pretty strange . . . in fact, pretty awful.

Or suck on a stick of fresh cloves. (We know it tastes bitter, but try it anyway; it is not fattening.) Now, right away, eat your favorite cream-filled cookie. We think you will not enjoy the taste of that cookie too much. We are sure that if you chew fresh cloves all the time, you would hardly ever want to eat cookies directly afterwards.

Dr. Plotz was really trying a much more complex and sophisticated form of the same experiment when he tested fifty patients to determine if the medicated gum for weight control containing benzocaine, combined with strong-tasting, aromatic ingredients, could help curb their appetite by altering their sense of taste.

These people were overweight from 12 to 102 pounds. They chewed the gum for ten weeks, one or two pieces before each meal, followed by a glass of water, as well as between meals—whenever they felt the urge to eat. They lost an average of two pounds per week, without any side effects, as reported by Dr. Plotz.

If two pounds a week seems like nothing to you, then you are thinking all wrong about your diet. Two pounds a week is regarded as a safe, effective rate of weight loss for a dieting adult. We pediatricians are concerned about interfering with adequate growth; therefore, we limit our weight loss expectations to one pound per week. This loss should be acceptable for many adults as well.

If you lose one pound a week for eight weeks you will be eight pounds lighter. (And 8 weeks is only the length of your summer vacation.) If you follow the Long Beach Diet for another eight weeks you may just be on your way to re-training your sense of taste so that you can reorganize your eating habits for life. Stick to it another eight weeks, and it may have become a way of life.

You may just be able to give up "Compensatory Overtasting."

The Long Beach Project: In the Beginning

As pediatricians doing our best to help mothers start their children off in life with healthy eating habits, it was comparatively easy to teach them how to deal with the problem while their children were babies. But by the time the babies were toddlers, and certainly by the time they were of kindergarten age, those youngsters knew all too well about such things as cakes, candies and similar seductive sweets. How were mothers to deal with children who, during the day, felt hungry and demanded

49

these things? And especially how could we help mothers whose children were already overweight and had bad eating habits? How could we wean those youngsters away from "junk food"?

Over the years we concocted the most delicious but healthy substitutes that we could imagine, which are described later. And yet we always wished that there were something simple and handy that would, at the right time, allow a child to ease the pang of a desire for something sweet (as candy does, without being a candy) something that would give an instant of pleasure and satisfaction.

One of us—it was Dr. Pisacano—had discovered a candy medication for weight control, and we decided to test this in clinical studies in our own offices.

Frequently, doctors are asked by medical companies to make such tests. However, reputable physicians would never agree unless they were as certain as they could be that the products were safe and the risks, if any, minimal. And even then they would not make such tests unless the patients (in this case, the parents), with full knowledge of what was involved, volunteered to participate.

The opportunity to test a candy medication for weight control appealed to us for one obvious reason. It is difficult enough to help adults cope with cravings for sweets. At least adults can be talked to, lectured, argued with or rebuked. But, as almost all parents are sadly aware, it is infinitely more difficult to use such approaches with little children who cannot be expected to understand the true nature of the problem.

After examining considerable research on previous tests conducted with these products, we felt that the ingredients they contained might succeed in curbing the sense of taste and therefore might curb excessive appetite. Most important, they might divert the desire for a sweet taste at just those moments when impulsive eating is about to begin.

Consequently, we went ahead and tested this weight control medicated gum with some encouraging results. In the course of the tests, referred to as the Long Beach Project, we examined some of the returns from a customer survey that had been taken among users of medicated candy for weight control. Some of the responses to this survey, which had been made originally by the manufacturer, seemed to warrant further checking. We contacted these people (Dorothy N. was one of them), interviewed them at some length, and received long letters from some of them in response to our note that we were gathering material for a book.

In this way, we were able to develop case studies of adults, in addition to the case studies of youngsters and their parents which had come from our own practice. We learned volumes about the eating patterns of grownups as they are derived from the tasting habits established in childhood.

Diet Double-Think: Damned If You Do, Damned If You Don't

One thing became dramatically clear to us in the course of our examination of the customer survey answers: women were much more concerned about dieting than men.

There were over thirty-five thousand answers to the survey, almost all of them stating that candy weight control medication had helped them lose some weight. But it was very interesting that less than two thousand of these answers came from men.

Why do women worry so much more about dieting than men do?

Women feel they have to be attractive, while men do not feel that need so keenly. Most diet advertising and diet aids are directed toward making women more desirable sex objects. "He will love you more if there is less of you" is the general theme of the low-calorie industry. Sugarless soda companies display photographs of bathing beauties with the admonition, "Keep America Beautiful." Yogurt companies feature a delicate slim girl who is being courted and kissed.

We sense a contradiction in the way the food problem is presented to the American woman. On one hand, she is told that if she eats yogurt or drinks diet soda, men will adore her. On the other hand, she is told that if she serves whipped cream topping on her scrumptious seven layer cakes or pours beer upon demand, men will also adore her.

Look at that contradiction. If a wife eats healthy, light foods and stays slim, she will be adored. If a wife feeds her husband unhealthy, fattening foods that will put a strain on his heart and shorten his life, she will be adored.

We call this "Diet Double-Think."

The definition of female beauty may be narrower than that male attractiveness. Fat men, even fat television heroes never quite get the girl. Fat teenage boys do not go out for football any more than fat teenage girls become cheerleaders. When summertime comes, fat men can think up as many excuses not to go to the beach as can fat women.

Nobody really seems to be looking out for the fat men, least of all the fat men themselves. The most likely people to do that job in our society are women. Women generally have it within their power to make America beautiful and healthy, because, no matter what reasons made them go on diets themselves, they are usually responsible for the eating habits of a number of other people in the family.

The Taste-Makers

Women generally decide how the market basket dollar will be spent and we learn to like what they bring home. In addition, women shape the taste of the young. The food they feed the children, will be what children will want to eat for the rest of their lives.

The absolute dependence of most Americans on the nutritional decisions of women is one of the most important aspects of the national diet dilemma.

This is guideline number five: One of the major safeguards of the nation's nutritional health lies in education in the basic principles of sensible eating.

Think of it. Most grown men in this country have never actually fed themselves for any length of time. When they were little, they were fed by mothers. When they were of high school age and their sisters were beginning to prepare meals, they were still being fed by their mothers and their sisters. When they left home, and became bachelors they probably lived on pre-cooked, pre-packaged foods. They knew little or nothing about the nutritional value of foods, and they were never encouraged to learn. The point is that millions of American men never make their own nutritional decisions; they eat what is prepared for them or what is most convenient to prepare.

Why do so many men gain weight after they marry? Because they are being fed three regular meals a day, probably for the first time since they left their mothers' homes. Once a man is married, the likelihood that he will ever feed himself again is directly related to the figures for divorce and widowhood. A happily married man whose wife is blessed with good health and long life could be as dependent as a baby forever.

This is one area from which men as well as women should be liberated. For one of the worst things about women always being in the kitchen is that men are always at the table.

It's time that both parents realized that feeding a whole group of people for a number of years is a family responsibility.

One mother once told us that she reaches for the medicated gum first when doing her weekly food shopping because it helps to modify her 'buying behavior,' preventing her from buying the "baddies," like potato chips and other junk foods.

Guideline number six: The taste-maker in the family has to find something else to be proud of other than the food they feed them.

Dorothy N's aunt, who smuggled the hamburgers to her husband in the hospital, was probably a devoted wife just trying to appease her husband's desires. If she had been a little less indulgent, he might be alive today.

In our pediatric practice, we always hold parents responsible for the overweight of their children.

If the parents are fat and the child is fat too, well, obviously overfeeding and overtasting are family problems. We prescribe the Long Beach Diet and try to re-educate the mothers, the taste-makers, on how they can re-educate the sense of taste of their families.

If the parents are slim and their child is fat, we have a long conference with both parents. We explain; we educate; we try to make parents see that it is wrong, not loving, for them to live carefully on salads and whole wheat toast while allowing their child to gorge themselves on calorie-loaded confections. In our practice, we make a point of enumerating these dangerous treats to our mothers.

The only way for a woman who is the feeder and the taste-maker for her family to meet her responsibility is for her to become informed about the basic principles of sensible eating and wed her feeding patterns firmly to the concept of taste control.

A whole new kind of shopping, a whole new awareness in cooking is required. An enlightened feeder, we believe, holds the key to this country's good health.

CHAPTER 3

Taste Control, In Your Practice And Ours

In our practice over the years, we have originated, evolved, and adapted some theories, which have shaped our thinking about how to control the lifetime eating habits of the growing human being.

Carbohydrate Control: An Ounce of Prevention

What is a carbohydrate?

In its simplest form, a carbohydrate is sugar. In its complex form, it is starch. Both sugar and starch supply energy. Carbohydrates comprise a great percentage of most of the common foods we eat. The most familiar carbohydrate is the refined, granulated sugar that too many people keep at hand on the table. Americans have the highest rate of sugar consumption in the world—up to 125 pounds per person per year compared with a world average of 25 pounds per person. That 125 pounds is an average, which means that there must be many people who consume more than the average. For example, infants and children as a class, in some sectors of society, sometimes consume up to the amazing level of 200 pounds of sugar annually!

To us, this is a horrifying statistic, because new research accuses sugar—especially ordinary white "table" sugar—of playing a part in just about every degenerative disease associated with the affluent society in which we live. Diabetes, heart disease, hardening of the arteries, cancer—these are the diseases we mean. When we look at the alarming increases in diabetes and obesity in the young people of America, we must wonder, "Why us? Why our country? What are we doing wrong?"

We have a theory about what we as a nation are doing wrong.

The pancreas, that fish-shaped gland inside your abdomen, secretes juices to aid your digestion, and also a hormone called insulin. Insulin is manufactured in special clusters of cells, scattered throughout the pancreas called the Islets of Langerhans. There are about a million islets in the pancreas. Each islet contains from a few to a hundred cells.

We believe that once an islet is destroyed, it is not replaced. Our theory is that these mini-manufacturing plants of insulin are finite in number, and that they can become exhausted.

Insulin is the hormone which helps make the sugar you eat available to each cell in the body, as fuel for the job that cell performs. Diabetes is a disease in which the body's insulin requirements are not met and sugar builds up in the blood, causing all types of havoc. Diabetes can be inherited, but the great increase in diabetes in the United States goes way beyond the expected inheritance factor. (In 1972, about two million people suffered from diabetes in America. In 1958, it was estimated that only about a hundred thousand suffered from this disease.)

Our theory is that nature made the islets in the pancreas capable of secreting enough insulin for more than the average lifetime of a human being, provided the sugar intake was within a reasonable amount, perhaps between twenty-five and fifty pounds per year. Not all the islets produce insulin at the same time, and production is geared to the demands of the body. Now if you multiply that twenty-five-pound sugar intake by eight, what happens? We affirm that you use up your islets and by the early adult years, sometimes sooner, you are a diabetic. Your pancreas is no longer capable of producing the necessary insulin.

There are two main ways in which non-hereditary diabetics develop diabetes. One is by living to a very old age, in which case you have outlived nature's plan for your pancreas. The second way is by overconsuming sugar. In the latter case, you have wilfully destroyed nature's plan.

We are convinced that too many people in this country are overeating carbohydrates, especially refined sugar.

We further theorize that the body has a few "tricks" to ensure the flow of fuel to its cells. It uses the sugar-insulin system for quick energy and it uses a fat-mobilizing-hormone system as an energy source for replenishment and, we believe, growth.

We grow when we sleep as children, and we replenish tired cells when we sleep as adults. We know from many studies that when insulin levels are low, free fats are high except in overweight people. Insulin seems to be the most needed, so it is the sugar-insulin system which receives priority in the body economy. Perhaps when a diet unbelievably rich in carbohydrates is the rule, there is so much sugar-insulin energy available, awake and asleep, that the body never gets a chance to use the fat. After all, we know that a high insulin level in the blood keeps fats from being released from their swollen storage cells, so the body uses the energy available, sugar energy, to do the job that fat was supposed to do. The fat then just remains in the body. The body economy forgets how to balance energy supply from sugar and from fat. We believe that a possible solution to childhood obesity lies in vastly reducing sugar intake in the early years, thereby making a child's metabolism function properly. We also believe that it is important to get a child's body used to processing fat for energy, thereby preventing overweight caused by fat storage. We think the Long Beach Diet, as a lifetime program, is one way for a mother to reduce her children's chances of "sugar seduction."

Although carbohydrates serve as a major source of energy, we think we've made the point that they should be avoided in large quantities. Not only do they contribute to a variety of diseases, but they tend to delay the elimination of water from the body's tissues, causing the body to retain fluids and keep weight on.

Fat Control: Quality vs. Quantity

Americans eat too much fat—too much saturated fat in particular. An average of 40 to 50 percent of the total calories in our average national diet comes from fat—dairy cream, vegetable fat, animal fat. We are convinced that the low, balanced polyunsaturated to saturated fat ratio of the Long Beach Diet, introduced early in life, teaches a baby's body how to burn up the fat in its fat storage (adipose) cells. That is why we put our babies on skim milk at about three to four months of age.

Look what happens. We notice a definite drop in the rate of weight gain following the transfer from formula to skim milk, but there is no decrease at all in the rate of height gain. And our babies thrive.

This means our skim milk babies are using the fat they have already stored to grow on. Their bodies are getting in the habit of metabolizing fat, moving it out of the storage cells and using it for energy on which to grow.

If a mother can cut down on the number of fat storage cells her baby develops in the active phase of growth, by cutting down on fat consumption, fewer cells in her child's body will hold an abnormal extra amount of fat. One ounce of fat cells that we can prevent an infant from forming might conceivably have held ten pounds of fat in the overweight adult.

Guideline number seven: One ounce of prevention is worth ten pounds of cure.

How Mother Can Control Eating Behavior

Mothers have absolute control over the eating habits of their families. We are completely convinced of this and we have proven it in our own practice.

When we have been able to help reorganize the feeding habits of mothers, they have brought back into our offices a whole generation of children who like salmon and yogurt and who do not eat or miss chocolate-flavored milk and fruit-flavored, sugared cereals, and who are on the right dietary road to good health.

We have many children in our own practice who have already developed the habit of being pacified with sweets after every setback. If they do not get on a team or they do not get a part in the school play, Mama pacifies their hurt feelings with an ice cream sundae. (It is the same syndrome that we saw when Dorothy N's grandmother gave her all that extra strawberry shortcake.) The trouble is, as these children grow older they grow more overweight. Fat children usually have difficulties socially, and they develop the need for more and more ice cream sundaes (or something equally sweet tasting) to make them feel better. Not just the mind, but the body itself has become attuned to emotional pacification through the taste of sweetness. This has become an ingrained response.

60

The mother who pacifies pain through fattening foods has completely misunderstood the "pleasure economy" of her child. She must, instead, help her child grow up to have a pleasure economy wherein he compensates himself for life's setbacks through some pleasure income that is not as dangerous as fattening foods. A mother must not encourage her child to use taste as compensation for emotional losses. And she should remember: she is the *only one* who can do this for her child.

Remember guideline number eight: Avoid oral gratification of emotional needs.

The Long Beach Project: How It Developed

Encouraged by the work of Dr. Plotz published in his article in the *Medical Times* and others, we were already convinced that taste control was the key to sugar and fat limitation in a diet. We knew that the taste for sweetness was epidemic in the taste buds of our countrymen, and that even the strongest-willed mother might need some help in establishing a new set of taste controls to use at her family table.

Consequently, we became interested in further clinical examination at our own offices on a product similar to the one tested by Dr. Plotz to help his overweight patients. Such a product was of interest to us for several reasons.

First, the product Dr. Plotz had used was not absorbed into the bodily system. It did not appear to cause any untoward side effects.

Second, Dr. Plotz made no claims that the product curbed the sense of taste, just that it seemed to assuage it for a while. We knew full well, as pediatricians, that any child who does not like his food is not going to stay on his diet. (We believe that you are the same way too, no matter how much pleasure deprivation you think you have to endure while dieting.) We were looking for something that would help curb the desire to overtaste, without being so powerful as to spoil the taste of food.

Third, the medicated gum that Dr. Plotz had used was not an expensive medication requiring a prescription.

We were hoping that this sort of product might offer our patients a double-edged sword in fighting over-weight and reorganizing their eating habits.

On the one hand, the product might help satisfy the craving for sweetness and all the emotional gratification we knew the taste of sweetness represented. On the other hand, we might be able to make the child's stomach full by following the gum with a noncaloric, temporary bulk. In this case, a glass of water was recommended.

We figured that if the benzocaine in the product, combined with highly aromatic and flavorful, taste-dominating essential oils, could serve to dull the sense of taste for a while, a child would have less desire to over-eat at his or her meal, and, most important, between meals.

Sweetness (the medicated candy or gum); Bulk (the water); Taste Control (the benzocaine plus taste-modifying essential oils)—if we could get this combination of assistance for our dieting children, then we—and our partners, their parents—might have solved our problem.

We had two big questions before trying out the gum in our own offices.

A lot of our patients wear braces and we did not want them chewing gum. (There were horrible visions of the orthodontists of Long Island marching vengefully into our offices and putting braces on us as punishment.)

Coincidentally, the same active ingredient found in the

gum was also available in the candy medication. We checked with our colleagues in the dental profession to see if the sugar in the lozenge formula would increase the danger of cavities; they told us that the danger of cavities was minimal, as long as the child did as he was told: drink a glass of water, using it to rinse his mouth after eating each candy. The water worked as a stomach-filler, but as pediatricians, we were equally concerned that the water worked to wash away the sugar residue that the lozenge might have left on the child's teeth.

We had twenty-six children in our program, ranging in age from six to ten. Every week for eight weeks, they came to our office for a check-up and an interview. At the first visit, we gave them the Long Beach Diet, a supply of medicated candy to help them stay on the diet, and instructions to drink a glass of water after eating each piece before and between meals. The Long Beach Diet we prescribed was the reducing version for children, approximately twelve hundred calories per day. They were not told the brand name of the product, so that they could make their own decisions as to its effectiveness independent of any advertising they might have seen. Every week, we gave pep talks—one for the children, and one for their mothers.

Without exception, the children liked the candy medication. Every mother admitted that it was not that difficult preparing meals within the guidelines of the Long Beach Diet. (Let's face it—it's no real chore to substitute vealburgers for hamburgers.)

The total weight loss of the twenty-six children was ninety-nine pounds in eight weeks, an average of 3.8 pounds per child. Almost one-third of the group lost between 5 and 10.5 pounds. Only two of the children gained weight—one gained half a pound, another 3.25

pounds. These two children and their mothers simply could not find the motivation to stay on the diet or even use the candy according to the instructions of the "Long Beach Project."

Twenty-four out of twenty-six children had shown they had acquired the self-discipline and increased motivation to reduce far beyond what might have been expected from their age group. At a time when children should be putting on weight and growing, these children were growing the right way—taller and thinner—not fatter. "I am so glad you gave us those (medicated) candies," one typical mother told us. "They really helped my child stay on her diet."

We know all the parents of the children in our Long Beach Project, and we knew a lot of them were fat. It was part of our dream that the lesson they learned for their children's sake would not be lost on them.

The Long Beach Diet is not some wild, miracle, fad diet "guaranteed" to make the fat melt like snow. In fact, it is not really a diet at all—it is a way of eating. For overweight people it is a way of losing weight if they use it in conjunction with taste control. For slender people, it is a way of staying slender. And for everyone, it is a way of eating more healthfully.

The Long Beach Diet is also a way of feeding. It is a guide to new, improved grocery shopping. We would like to see it attached to supermarket carts like a license plate. To us, the guidelines of the Long Beach Diet are as vital an aid to the consumer as unit pricing.

The Four Principles of the Long Beach Diet

1. You can take a lot of fat off your table without even noticing that it is gone.

Most animal protein foods contain a high proportion

of saturated fat. There are more than twice as many fat calories as there are protein calories in eggs, hamburgers, frankfurters, cold cuts, whole milk, and whole milk products. With rich cakes and pies, there are even more. Of the total calories in a piece of ordinary layer cake, made with whole milk and eggs and butter cream icing, 75 percent are fat calories.

So cut out very fat meat, such as bacon, sausage, pastrami, corned beef, and hot dogs.

You cannot eat eggs without bacon, you say? Fine, then cut down on both. In our opinion nobody needs more than four eggs a week.

If you crave the taste of delicatessen food, try chicken and turkey roll or slices.

2. Give up milk and whole milk products as much as you possibly can—the taste adjustment will be minimal.

Whole milk products include butter, cream, ice cream and cream cheese. The only margarine that is low enough in fat for the Long Beach Dieter to use is that made with vegetable oils. The only salad oil you should use is vegetable oil—corn oil, for example, but definitely not coconut oil. Neither do we recommend peanut oil.

As people grow older, their bodies tend to have greater difficulty processing the lactose in whole milk. Mysteriously enough, a wondrous taste adjustment takes place to make this metabolic change easier to deal with. You do not seem to enjoy the taste of milk as much when you are forty as you did when you were fourteen. Research has shown that millions of adults simply cannot digest whole milk after childhood. In certain ethnic groups, this is even more pronounced. Among Jews of European ancestry and certain Black and Oriental populations, a very high percentage are reported unable to digest whole milk as adults. Whole milk may actually be unhealthy for these people who suffer from stomach and intestinal distress when they drink it.

If you look a little more closely at your dairy counter, you will see that virtually all the whole milk products you use frequently can be substituted with skim milk products, with no less taste pleasure, and probably equal satisfaction for your appetite.

3. If your idea of dessert is cake, pastry, cream-filled cookies, doughnuts and other elaborate confections, either eliminate dessert or change your idea.

Dessert is a taste habit, a tradition, a delight to the eye and to the palate, but we think nine out of ten people really do not expect it, and certainly do not need the extra calories. Save it for special occasions if you must.

If you have to sweeten food with sugar to make it palatable, then do not serve such food at all!

If dessert is absolutely necessary to you, then serve fresh fruit, cheese, cookies that do not have cream in the middle, fresh frozen fruit dessert, angel food or sponge cake or almond macaroons.

And if you must serve dessert, reserve it for the bedtime snack.

4. Take the salt shaker off the table.

We have no doubt that you seasoned your dinner well enough when you cooked it. Children need not get into the habit of improving on a good thing by adding more salt to pre-salted food. There is substantial evidence to indicate that excess salt intake contributes to eventual hypertension.

Seven Ways to Cultivate Proper Taste

1. Lean meat.

Trim off all the visible fat. There is more lurking inside that thick red steak, but it is nowhere near as much as you will eat if you do not trim your beef lean.

Keep your portions moderate: 4 to 6 ounces before cooking, 4 ounces at the most after cooking. (If 4 ounces does not seem like much to you, remember it is your palate that is telling you. Four ounces is plenty, and if you will really listen—to the full signals from your stomach, you will know it is sufficient.)

For seven lunches and seven dinners per week, eat fish and shellfish, poultry and veal at ten of them, and beef, pork, lamb and organ meats (like liver) at the other four meals. (Shellfish is low in calories but fairly high in cholesterol, so that it should be eaten sparingly).

2. Eggs in moderation.

We recommend four or fewer eggs per week for all age levels. Even though eggs are high in protein, they are also high in cholesterol, and while they are a traditional part of our national diet, they should be eaten in moderation.

3. Skim milk and milk products.

We admit there is a taste difference between skim and whole milk. We believe it is mostly a matter of texture, But in other skim milk/whole trade-offs, the taste difference is not so apparent at all. In some cheeses, American processed cheese or cottage cheese, for example, there is very little taste difference between the whole and the skim milk varieties. For example, we recommend Jarlsberg rather than whole milk Swiss cheese.

In cooking, we can see no difference at all in most dishes. Mozzarella melts over pasta just as scrumptiously if it is made from skim or whole milk. Blintzes taste just as good with skim milk cottage cheese inside them as they do with whole milk cottage cheese. Cake mix blends just as nicely with skim as with whole. You can even scald skim milk, when a recipe calls for it as easily as you can whole milk.

We recommend two cups of skim milk daily for adults

who want milk, two to four cups for children. No more! Drink water!

If you adhere to our recommended skim milk intake and cook with skim milk, you will cut down considerably on fat intake and help yourself to lose weight without sacrificing the pleasure you get from the good taste of food. Ounce for ounce, whole milk has 50% more calories than skim milk and 700% more fat.

4. Vegetables and fruits.

If you never developed a taste for these, do it now— the sooner the better.

You should eat raw or cooked fruits and vegetables every day. If you have a garden plot or even a couple of planters on a city terrace, grow one or two vegetables.. You are likely to eat them if you grow them, if only as a matter of horticultural pride.

Remember, a filling for your stomach is not necessarily the same as the filling for an eclair! You can get sufficient amounts to eat with fresh fruit and vegetables. The fiber is good for you too.

5. Whole grain breads and cereals.

All enriched whole grain breads and cereals are fine for you and your children, however, we discourage eating double decker sandwiches.

6. Light desserts . . . if you must.

Ask your bakery for cakes and pastry made with liquid vegetable shortening only.

Try gelatin desserts with fruit or natural sherbet.

If you must have a topping, because your taste buds have been trained to respond to them, then make it with evaporated milk, dry skim milk, or yogurt.

Try John's Ambrosia. Take one package of flavored low-calorie gelatin dessert. Add equal parts of water and unsweetened fruit juice, increasing the recommended amount of liquid by one half. Prepare as for all gelatins, and chill. When partially set, add your own fresh diced fruit mixture. Chill again until set. Spoon this into a parfait glass alternately with plain or fruit-flavored yogurt or whipped skim milk. Now eat the gorgeous creation, very slowly.

And for lunch, we suggest you try Henry's Zuppa à la Fromage. Put a mound of pot cheese, seasoned or plain into a dish. Boil a cupful of bouillon and pour it over the cheese. Eat, with a teaspoon.

7. A note on yogurt and fish.

Of all the tastes that Americans seem to neglect, and which the rest of the whole world long ago learned to relish, the two which we find foreign to the American palate are fish and yogurt.

Fish is the backbone of many a sensible diet. If your mother never served it and you never learned to like it, learn now. If you are a mother, now is the time to get your children used to it, so that they will eat it with zest throughout life. Fish is very high in protein, and with a few exceptions very low in saturated fat, and low in calories. Serve it as plain as you can. Do not fry it. Instead, season it with lemon, broil, and enjoy the natural fish flavor.

As for yogurt, John's Ambrosia is proof that yogurt can, with a little effort, pass for whipped cream any time. Remember, you are in a deadly serious battle to outwit your mis-trained sense of taste! If it looks like whipped cream, your taste buds will get excited about it as surely as the dogs in Pavlov's famous experiment got excited about their food the minute the dinner bell was heard. So let your taste buds get excited about something disguised as whipped cream, which, like yogurt, is actually good for you!

Dr. John and Dr. Henry's LONG BEACH DIET MENU is . . .

A prescribed set of meals which is tasty, nutritious and low-calorie—less than 1600 calories per day. The menus follow the weight loss guidelines of the principles outlined in this book and can be varied by exchanging one food for another of caloric equivalence which you will find listed in the handy Long Beach Diet Exchange on page 99 .

Do not eat anything between meals, *except* for a medicated chewing gum or a medicated candy* to help curb your sweet tooth and stick to the diet program. Use this helpful tool instead of snacks or dessert along with a liquid to slightly modify your taste sensations and curb the wild cravings for excess foods that you often can't control. These delicious aids will help you diet sensibly to achieve your weight loss goal.

We are giving you the opportunity to have your taste buds experience the exotic and perhaps unfamiliar flavors of low calorie culinary delights. We are trying to wean you from the appeal of rich, high caloric sauces and dressings to the tempting and equally delicious, well balanced, and fulfilling flavors available to the thoughtful cook. If you can eliminate a large number of calories here and there, then you will reach your goal sooner. 1200 calories is the recommended amount to shed those unwanted pounds and to accustom your body to require less food. Our menus vary somewhere between 1200 and 1600 calories to give you an idea of the variety of foods that can be enjoyed while trying to lose weight. It's a

*We recommend Slim-Line Candy or Slim-Mint Chewing Gum, products of the Thompson Medical Company, New York, New York.

good idea to check with your doctor, before beginning a diet of any kind.

Once the general idea of how the Long Beach Diet works is clear to you, then by all means, be creative. Make up a diet that suits your own taste preferences and which you can live with comfortably the rest of your life.

FIRST WEEK

Day One

BREAKFAST	*CALORIES*
¾ cup strawberries with	
½ cup skim milk	90
6 silver dollar pancakes with 1 tablespoon	
maple syrup*	180
coffee (you may stir your coffee with the spoon you used	
for the maple syrup)	00

Total calories	270

* When making pancakes, be sure to use vegetable oil, margarine, skim milk and only one egg—if you need more egginess, add another egg white, and use a very hot teflon pan with no grease.

LUNCH	*CALORIES*
Deep dish salmon pie**	295
2 cups of salad with low-calorie dressing	50
Mocha Angel cake, 1 slice***	130

Total calories	475

** Deep dish salmon pie was invented by a mother we know. She took three ounces of salmon from a can (120 calories), added two stiffly beaten egg whites and ½ cup skim milk cottage cheese (100 calories) and ½ teaspoon baking powder. She seasoned with parsley, pepper and salt. Then she poured the mixture into a greased baking dish (1½ teaspoon of margarine) adding only 50 calories and baked it in little crocks in a 400 degree oven until it was brown and crispy. A great hot lunch—to be served the minute it comes from the oven, like a souffle. *** Prepare angel food cake mix as directed on package except stir 1 tablespoon powdered instant coffee into the dry mix before folding in egg whites. Top each slice with ¼ cup cut-up fresh peaches and a sprinkling of nutmeg. 16 servings (130 calories each).

DINNER	*CALORIES*
6 ounces of broiled lean beef, with	
all fat trimmed off	370
½ cup rice mixed	100
with ¼ cup peas mixed	30
with 1 tablespoon margarine	100
green salad with radishes,	
low-calorie dressing	50
2 slices canned pineapple (3 oz.)	
—pineapple in its own juice,	
not syrup or fresh pineapple	55

Total calories 705
Sauce   50

Grand Caloric total 1500

If a sauce is desired for variety:

a. 1 cup of mushrooms (approximately 50 calories); sauté in ½ tblsp. butter (optional) and smother your steak:

b. Aunt Sylvia's Old South Steak Sauce (can be saved in refrigerator).

In a sauce pan, combine ½ stick of margarine

2 cut-up onions   2 green peppers

½ bottle of catsup   1 cup fresh sliced mushrooms

½ bottle of water

Stir ingredients, cook on medium heat until peppers are soft. Serve hot over the steak. It is so delicious you'll want to try it again on next week's steak. This can serve 6 people: 2 tbsps. will provide about 50 calories.

8:30 p.m.: TV time and time for some candy medication for weight control as a snack. These will help you through those more difficult "hungry hours"—the times when you normally reach for a fattening piece of cake or candy.

Day Two

BREAKFAST	CALORIES
1 sliced orange	70
1 cup dry cereal	
with 1 cup skim milk	190
1 cup black coffee	00
1 piece whole wheat toast	55
1 teaspoon margarine	30

Total calories 345

LUNCH	CALORIES
3 oz. apple juice	47
English muffin pizza*	350
Coffee or tea	0

Total calories 397

* English Muffin Pizza
English muffin or 2 thinly sliced large pieces of
Italian Bread
4 slices of part skim milk mozzarella ⅛" thick,
tomato sauce, oregano, garlic salt
Lightly toast muffin or bread. Place enough cheese
to cover muffin. Spread sauce over cheese. Season
with oregano and garlic salt to taste. Shred remaining
mozzarella and sprinkle over sauce. Bake until bubbly.

DINNER	CALORIES
Kung Fu Shrimp and Mushrooms*	220
2 cups mixed green salad with	
low calorie dressing	50
1 slice whole wheat bread	55

Jan's Fresh Fruit delight**   150
2 oatmeal cookies   240
                                                          _____
                          Total Calories 715
                          Grand caloric total 1457

*   Kung Fu Shrimp and Mushrooms
2 tablespoons   sesame oil
2 cups diced celery
1 can (6oz.) sliced mushrooms drained,
    or fresh mushrooms
3 tablespoons soy sauce
1 teaspoon ginger
⅛ teaspoon Cayenne pepper (if you like it hot);
    otherwise, black pepper
1 clove minced garlic
1 minced scallion
2 cans (4½ oz. each) shrimp, rinsed
    and drained, or fresh shrimp.
2 cups hot cooked rice
In wok or large skillet prepare sesame oil by heating
with soy sauce, ginger, pepper, garlic, and scallion.
When garlic is lightly browned add mushrooms and celery, stirring until completely coated with sesame-spice
mixture (2 to 3 minutes). Stir in shrimp and cook
another few minutes until shrimp are heated
thoroughly. Spoon each serving over ½ cup of hot rice.
4 servings (220 calories each serving).

** Jan's Fresh Fruit Delight
    We use two of each of the following:
    grapefruit, eating oranges, pears, apples, bananas,
    and another fruit in season. Lemon Juice if more
    liquid is required. Cut and section grapefruit and
    oranges, removing all pulp and seeds. Cut grapefruit

and oranges in half. Free each segment from its pulp Place segments in a large bowl. Squeeze juice from emptied half into the bowl. Dice the other fruit and add to citrus mixture, stirring so that all fruit is covered with citrus juice. Have one cup for dessert and save the rest for another meal.

Day Three

BREAKFAST	CALORIES
½ glass orange juice	60
1 egg boiled or poached	80
1 slice whole wheat bread	55
1 teaspoon margarine	30
1 glass skim milk	85
coffee	00

Total calories 310

LUNCH	CALORIES
Halibut with vegetables*	180
1 slice whole wheat bread	55
Rice pudding Royale**	112
Coffee or tea	00

Total calories 347

* Halibut with vegetables

2 lbs. halibut fillets	3 stalks celery
1 teaspoon salt	6 green onions
¼ teaspoon pepper	1 teaspoon salt
¼ teaspoon paprika	1 tablespoon lemon juice
2 carrots	

Heat oven to 350°. Place fish in ungreased baking dish or pan 13 x 9 x 2 inches. Season with 1 teaspoon salt, pepper and paprika.
Cut carrots, celery and onions (with tops) into 1-inch lengths. Place in blender. Add enough water to cover. Chop watching carefully. Drain thoroughly. (Carrots can be shredded and celery and onions chopped finely by hand.)

Spread vegetables on fish, season with 1 teaspoon salt. Sprinkle with lemon juice. Cover, bake 30 minutes or until fish flakes easily with fork. 6 servings—180 calories each.

** Rice Pudding Royale
1 cup skim milk
½ cup uncooked long grain rice
1/3 cup sugar
½ teaspoon grated lemon peel
¼ teaspoon grated orange peel
1 teaspoon vanilla
¼ teaspoon almond extract
¾ cup cream style cottage cheese

In top of double boiler, combine milk and 2 cups water, add rice, sugar and ¼ teaspoon salt. Cook, covered over boiling water for 1 hour, stir often. Uncover, cook till thickened, 30 to 40 minutes. Remove from heat, stir in grated peels and flavorings. Chill thoroughly. Beat cottage cheese, stir into rice mixture. Spoon into dessert dishes, sprinkle with shredded orange peel, if desired. Makes 8 servings—112 calories per serving.

DINNER	CALORIES
8 oz. portion Mama Maggie's Spaghetti and Meat balls*	300
½ oz. Parmesan cheese	65
green salad	50
2 bread sticks	50
apple	70
coffee or tea	00
Total calories	535
Grand caloric total	1,192

* Mama Maggie's Spaghetti and Meatballs

Spaghetti; any type of pasta you like. They are all approximately equal in caloric content. The high protein variety contains less starch. All pasta *must* be cooked "al dente."

Tomato Sauce:

2 tablespoons olive oil
1 clove garlic, crushed
1 small chopped onion
6 medium-sized ripe tomatoes (cut in eighths)
1 6 oz. can tomato puree
1 whole bay leaf
½ teaspoon basil leaf (minced)
½ teaspoon oregano
1 teaspoon parsley flakes
½ teaspoon pepper

Place oil, onion, parsley and garlic in sauce pan. Brown lightly. Add tomatoes, puree, pepper, and cracked bay leaf and simmer gently for 45 minutes. Stir occasionally. Add basil and oregano and cook for ten minutes longer. This will make enough sauce for 1 pound of spaghetti. It may be refrigerated or frozen for future use.

Meatballs:

1 lb. lean chopped meat—beef
   or veal, or a mixture of both.
½ medium minced onion
1 egg
½ teaspoon parsley flakes
1 small minced garlic clove
1 teaspoon parmesan cheese
1 quarter teaspoon basil
1 quarter teaspoon oregano
1 slice favorite soft or no crust bread, soaked in water.
1/3 cup bread crumbs (omit if hard-crusted Italian bread is used).

Squeeze all water from wet bread. Place all ingredients in a large mixing bowl. Mix well by hand; but do not press meat mixture. Shape lightly into your favorite size meatballs. Cook in either way: sauté in teflon pan turning frequently until brown and firm.

Place on ungreased cookie sheet cook in 350° oven, undisturbed for 20 minutes.

Set meatballs aside.

When pasta is done "al dente" your dinner is ready to be served.

(Meatballs may be placed in the sauce while the spaghetti is cooking if you desire.)

Day Four

BREAKFAST	CALORIES
¾ cup orange juice *	90
2 slices whole grain toast	110
1 tablespoon margarine	100
1 cup skim milk	90
coffee	00
Total calories	390

* The pulp in freshly squeezed citrus juices doesn't add calories but it makes the juice much "meatier," creating a sensation of greater fullness than does the pulpless kind.

LUNCH	CALORIES
3 ounces boned chicken breast Lemon Baked Chicken Cutlet*	225
½ head lettuce and one medium tomato	50
1 tablespoon mayonnaise	110
1 biscuit, 2 inches in diameter	100
½ cup fruit cocktail	110
Total calories	595

* Lemon Baked Chicken:
Heat oven to 425. Remove skin from ¼ pound chicken breast. Split breast and place chicken in ungreased baking pan 9 x 9 x 2 inches. Spread 1 teaspoon soft butter or margarine on chicken. Sprinkle with ½ teaspoon salt and ¼ teaspoon paprika. Drizzle with lemon juice. Bake uncovered 35 to 45 minutes or until tender. Sprinkle with 2 tablespoons snipped parsley—225 calories.

DINNER	*CALORIES*
1 4-ounce vealburger	230
1 serving Middle Eastern Cucumber Salad*	100
½ cup macaroni—dusted with	
grated cheese of choice.	110
½ cup peas	60
sliced pear	100

Total Calories 600

* Middle Eastern Cucumber Salad—slice one medium cucumber and chop a scallion and mix with ½ cup plain yogurt and seasoning to taste. (We like salt and pepper and fresh dill.) This recipe should be more than adequate for two grown people.

Note: John usually finishes a second portion of cucumber salad around 10 o'clock at night with a cup of coffee, but that adds another 100 calories. A lower calorie idea is to take one or two medicated candies for weight control with a glass of water, or a cup of coffee or tea. The Slim-Line candies are delicious and will provide you with a great snack for those long evenings, and help you eliminate your craving for higher calorie snacks and desserts.

Grand caloric total 1585

Day Five

BREAKFAST	CALORIES
¾ cup orange juice	90
1 piece of toast	65
with ½ tablespoon margarine	50
1 cup whole grain cereal	95
with 1 cup skim milk	90
coffee	00

Total calories 390

LUNCH	CALORIES
Personalized Chow Mein*	625
1 cup green salad with no-calorie dressing	15
3 oz. apple juice, on ice	47

Total calories 687

* Personalized Chow Mein is your creation from some of the leftovers from your first days of Prudent Dieting:

1. 3 ounces of diced chicken left over (155 calories) or 3 ounces of cubed round roast (185 calories), etc.
2. ½ cup shredded cabbage (30 calories)
3. ½ cup green onion (40 calories)
4. 1 chicken or beef bouillon cube dissolved in 1 cup water (8 calories)
5. 1 tablespoon margarine (100 calories)

Add 1/3 cup sliced fresh mushrooms (15 calories) and/or 1/3 cup peas (15 calories) or any other leftover vegetable. Sauté the onion and mushrooms (if you're using them) in the margarine; add the bouillon and all the other vegetables, cover and cook *on a low fire*. After 15 minutes, add the chicken or beef and 2 tablespoons of

"Duck Sauce" (about 90 calories). If necessary add water. Adjust seasoning to taste. Serve over your rice with soy sauce (if desired) and eat very slowly.

DINNER	CALORIES
Baked rolled fillet of flounder*	140
2/3 cup corn	135
1 cup green beans	25
orange cauliflower salad**	50
2 bread sticks	50
Total calories	400

* Roll flounder fillet around a 3 inch length of the thick end of a scallion that has been rolled in mayonnaise. (It takes about 1 tablespoon [90 calories] of mayonnaise to coat 6 scallion pieces.) Season with salt, pepper, lemon juice; add ½ cup of water; sprinkle with parsley and paprika and bake for 20 minutes. A full 6 ounces of fish—300 calories.

** Orange cauliflower salad—
2 large tangerines, separated into segments, or
2 cans (10½ ounces each unsweetened
mandarin orange segments, drained
2 cups uncooked cauliflowerets
¼ cup chopped green pepper
2 cups bite size pieces spinach (about 2 ounces)
¼ cup low-calorie French salad dressing or Orange Blossom Dressing***

Toss orange segments, cauliflowerets, green pepper, spinach and salad dressing, 6 servings (50 calories each)
*** Orange Blossom Dressing: In covered jar, shake 1 can (14 ounces) evaporated skim milk and 1 can (6

ounces) thawed frozen orange juice concentrate until well mixed. 2 cups dressing (20 calories per tablespoon).

Grand caloric total 1477

For the Sixth and Seventh days of Long Beach Diet, try creating your own menus from the exchange list that follows remembering to include the Basic Four that all good nutritionists insist upon.

Dairy Products: 2 to 4 servings

Meat: 2 servings,—including poultry, fish and eggs

Vegetable and fruit: 4 servings (1 or 2 citrus)

Breads and cereal: 4 servings, including pasta and rice.

SECOND WEEK

Day One

BREAKFAST	CALORIES
½ medium cantaloupe	40
boiled or poached egg	80
1 slice wheat toast	55
1 tsp. margarine	30
coffee or tea	00
Total calories	205

LUNCH	CALORIES
Peach Sauced Ham *	217
½ cup green beans	30
1 slice whole wheat bread	55
coffee or tea	00
½ cup rice	94
Total calories	396

* Peach Sauced Ham
Trim fat from 1 fully cooked ham slice, 1 inch thick (about 2 pounds); slash ham edges at one-inch intervals. Place on broiler pan. Broil 3 inches from heat for 7 to 8 minutes, turn. Broil 5 to 6 minutes longer. Meanwhile, drain one 16 ounce can dietetic pack peach slices reserving ½ cup liquid. In saucepan blend reserved peach liquid with 1 tablespoon cornstarch and ¼ teaspoon ground cloves. Stir in 1 teaspoon shredded orange peel and ½ cup orange juice. Cook, stirring constantly till mixture thickens and bubbles, add peach slices. Heat thoroughly. Serve peach sauce on ham. Makes 8 servings—217 calories each.

DINNER	CALORIES
1 cup tomato juice	48
6 ounces roast chicken*	310
1 cup squash	35
1 cup spinach	45
1 cup mixed carrot and celery sticks and	
1 tablespoon mayonnaise for dipping	115
4 meringue cookies**	80
coffee	00

Total calories 633

*Place roasting chicken seasoned with salt, pepper and paprika, breast down in pan. Add 1 cup water and 2 quartered onions. Keep basting, adding water as needed. Optional spices may be added to the onion-water baste according to taste. Cook for about 1½ hours during the last half hour, turn chicken breastside up; let brown, adding more paprika if desired. Continue basting until ready to serve.

** Meringue Cookies

3 egg whites	¼ teaspoon salt
1 cup sugar	1 teaspoon vanilla

Heat oven to 300°. Blend egg whites, sugar, salt and vanilla in top of double boiler. Place over boiling water; beat with rotary beater, scraping bottom and sides of pan occasionally, until mixture forms stiff peaks. Drop mixture by teaspoonfuls onto 2 lightly greased baking sheets. (Drop all mixture onto the 2 baking sheets; bake only 1 baking sheet at a time.) Bake 12 to 15 minutes or until light brown. Immediately remove from baking sheet. 3½ dozen cookies—20 calories each.

Grand caloric total 1234

Day Two

BREAKFAST	CALORIES
½ medium grapefruit	50
1 poached egg placed on
... 1 piece whole wheat toast	135
1 cup skim milk	90
Black coffee	00
Total calories	275

LUNCH	CALORIES
Uncle John's calzone*	200
2 cups mixed green salad	30
(no-calorie dressing: Lemon Juice, pepper,
salt, or garlic salt and vinegar)
1 3 oz. serving sliced peaches
(fresh or in own juice)	45
Total calories	275

* Uncle John's calzone
Into pita bread fill with the following:
½ pot cheese, ½ part skim milk ricotta, a few diced pieces of part skim milk mozzarella cheese, close opening with tooth picks, heat in roaster oven until hot and juicy.

DINNER	CALORIES
½ cantaloupe	40
Lamb chops with vegetables*	240
(for that Chinese touch serve over ½ cup rice)	94
1 large oatmeal cookie	114
1 glass skim milk	90

Total calories 578

Grand caloric total 1,128

* Lamb Chops with Vegetables

4 shoulder lamb chops
(1 inch thick)
1 can (16 ounces) Chinese
vegetables, drained (reserve liquid)
1 can (8 ounces) water chestnuts,
drained, slice thinly (reserve liquid)
3 tablespoons soy sauce
2 beef bouillon cubes
1 clove garlic, minced
1 medium onion, sliced
2 tablespoons cornstarch
¼ cup water
1 green pepper, cut into strips
4 cherry tomatoes

Trim excess fat from meat. Lightly grease large skillet
with excess fat, brown meat. Drain off fat. Measure reserved vegetable liquid; if necessary, add water to measure ¾ cup liquid. Stir liquid, soy sauce, boullion cubes
and garlic into skillet, heat to boiling. Reduce heat. Add
onion, cover and simmer 30 minutes or until meat is
tender. Remove meat.
Blend cornstarch and water, stir gradually into skillet.
Cook stirring constantly, until mixture thickens and boils.
Boil and stir for 1 minute. Stir in green pepper, Chinese
vegetables and water chestnuts. Add meat and tomatoes.
Cover and simmer 10 minutes. 4 servings—240 calories
each.

Day Three

BREAKFAST | CALORIES
½ medium cantaloupe | 40
egg, any way you like it | 80
(may fry in teflon pan—Franny's Rocky Mountain Toast)*
1 slice of toast | 65
1 tsp. margarine | 30
coffee | 00

Total calories 215

* Franny's Rocky Mountain Toast
  1 piece favorite bread
  1 egg

Make a hole in the center of bread (size of juice glass); place bread in skillet with a small amount of margarine (if using teflon pan none is needed) crack egg and place in the hole in center of bread (white may overflow onto bread). Brown on one side and as egg hardens turn over and brown on other side. Serve when browned as desired.

LUNCH | CALORIES
1 cup tomato juice | 48
1 small can tuna, packed in water, served on | 127
2 cups mixed green salad with 2 tablespoons | 150
French Dressing: Mix 2 tablespoons low-calorie mayonnaise and
1 tablespoon catsup
adjust flavor and consistency to taste
2 bread sticks | 50

Total calories 375

DINNER	CALORIES
Curried Chicken*	249
½ cup rice	94
Green salad	50
1 cup cooked carrots	45
1 slice whole wheat bread	55
an apple	70

Total calories 563

Grand caloric total 1,153

* Curried Chicken

In skillet combine ½ cup water, ½ cup vegetable juice cocktail, and 1 crushed chicken boullion cube. Add one 2-2½ pound ready to cook broiler/fryer chicken, cut up and skinned, ½ cup chopped onion, 1 teaspoon curry powder, ½ teaspoon poultry seasoning, ½ teaspoon salt, and a dash of pepper. Cover and simmer 45 minutes. Remove chicken, skim off fat.

Blend 1 cup additional vegetable juice cocktail with 1 tablespoon all purpose flour, add to skillet. Cook and stir till thick and bubbly. Return chicken to sauce, top with 6½ ounce can unsweetened grapefruit sections, drained. Cover and heat thoroughly. Makes 4 servings—249 calories each.

BREAKFAST	CALORIES
½ medium grapefruit	50
1 piece whole grain toast	55
½ tablespoon corn oil margarine	50
1 cup whole grain cereal	95
1 cup skim milk	90
black coffee	00

(If you don't like your coffee black, put a little of the skim milk in it.)

Total calories 340

LUNCH	CALORIES
Chicken or beef bouillon, 1 cup	10
1 piece of toast	65
½ cup skim milk cottage cheese	110
1 apple	70
coffee or tea	00

Total calories 255

(Remember, Henry mixes his cheese into broth and brings the now great soup to a boil. Using an onion-flavor bouillion this creation can rival a good French onion soup. He also slices his apple sliver-thin and eats only one slice at a time.)

DINNER	CALORIES
1 cup tomato juice	48
6 ounces broiled fish—Creole Flounder*	207
medium baked potato	100
1 cup carrots	45
2 cups mixed green salad with no-calorie dressing	30

¾ cup John's Ambrosia   200

                          Total calories 630

                          Grand caloric total 1,225

* Creole Flounder
2 lbs. flounder or pollack fillets
1½ cups chopped tomatoes
½ cup chopped green pepper
1/3 cup lemon juice
1 tablespoon salad oil
2 teaspoons salt
2 teaspoons minced onion
1 teaspoon basil leaves
¼ teaspoon coarsely ground black pepper
4 drops red pepper sauce
green pepper rings

Heat oven to 500°. Place fillets in single layer in baking
dish 13½ x 9 x 2 inches. Stir together remaining ingredients except pepper rings; spoon over fillets.. Bake 5 to
8 minutes or until fish flakes easily with fork. Remove
fillets to a warm platter. Garnish with green pepper
rings. 4 to 6 servings.

If you need a snack in the middle of the afternoon, let
your taste sensations savor the great fruit flavors of the
candy medications for weight control. Take one or two
with a cup of coffee or tea, and you'll feel satisfied until
dinner.

Day Five

BREAKFAST	CALORIES
1 cup tomato juice	48
2 slices whole wheat toast	110
1 tbs. corn oil margarine	100
1 cup skim milk	90
coffee	00

Total calories 348

LUNCH	CALORIES
Egg Foo Yong*	
(two 5-inch patties)	220
fresh fruit cup (from leftovers)	150
2 bread sticks	50
cup of tea	00

Total calories 420

DINNER	CALORIES
4 oz. beef or veal roast	200
6 asparagus spears	40
1 medium baked potato	100
2/3 cup beets	50
1 plain cup cake	170
coffee or tea	00

Total calories 560

Grand caloric total 1,328

* Egg Foo Yong
1 tablespoon salad oil
1 medium chopped green pepper

1 medium onion, chopped
1 cup cleaned cooked shrimp, chopped
1 cup bean sprouts, rinsed and drained
1 tablespoon salad oil
Hot soy sauce**
1 8 oz. can water chestnuts,
drained and sliced
2 to 3 tablespoons soy sauce
5 eggs

In skillet, heat 1 tablespoon salad oil, cook and stir green pepper and onion until tender. Stir in shrimp, bean sprouts, water chestnuts and soy sauce. Heat through, remove from heat.
In bowl beat eggs until thick and lemon colored. Stir in shrimp mixture. In skillet heat 1 tablespoon salad oil, pour egg mixture into hot skillet from ladle or cup to form patties about 5 inches in diameter. When patties are set and brown, turn and brown other side.

Serve warm with Hot soy sauce. About eight 5-inch patties— 110 calories each.

** Hot soy sauce
Heat 2 cups beef bouillon to boiling. Blend 2 tablespoons cornstarch, ¼ cup cold water and 2 tablespoons soy sauce, stir gradually into bouillon. Cook stirring constantly, until mixture thickens and boils. Boil and stir 1 minute. About 2¼ cups sauce (5 calories per tablespoon).

We invite you to seek the aid of your spice rack. Imaginative use of spices can create the glamour and gourmet touch that will transform your basic diet into the exotic:

Garlic and oregano with tomatoes will make your dish "Italian."

Curry powder transports you to India.

Creole seasoning brings into your home a touch of Mardi Gras.

Following these suggestions, can help you overcome the worst enemy of your will power—BOREDOM.

The Long Beach Diet
Calorie Exchange

There are two kinds of foods the average person eats—foods for every day, and those for once-in-a-while. Everyday foods can be made interesting, depending on how you prepare them. The big difference between them and the foods you eat once-in-a-while is that the latter are relatively high in fat, sugar and calories.

With the use of our exchange list, you can plan your own daily meals to be as interesting as those we have prepared for you, simply by matching different foods of similar caloric values. For example, where we recommend vealburger, you might wish to substitute roast chicken. If the daily caloric tally does not exceed 1600 calories, you are within an acceptable limit. The key to feeling adequately fed on the Long Beach Diet is to eat lots of vegetables. Therefore, we have made our vegetable servings more generous than the usual one-half cup.

In addition, we have included a section entitled "Fixings," in order to get you to *cook* and to become aware of the calories ordinary condiments and cooking ingredients add to your food. Cook creatively, with condiments such as lemon juice, spices, fresh mint and yogurt. In this way you will learn to make the basically nonfattening list of foods as delicious as any once-in-a-while dish. Besides, cooking (and the smelling and tasting that goes with it) is an appealing part of eating, a "first course" that can make you less hungry when you finally sit down to eat. Cooking certainly keeps you involved with your food longer, makes your meals more interesting and creates a focal point for conversation. Finally, if you were an imaginative cook before you started eating according to the guidelines of the Long Beach Diet, you will want to continue your creativity with food even more. With our exchange list, see what you can create out of it. We are sure you can make a lifetime of good eating for yourself and your family.

Calorie Chart

Poultry	Calories
¼ chicken, broiled	115
3 ounces white meat chicken, roast, broiled, boiled	115
4 ounces white meat turkey	215
4 ounces white and dark meat turkey	246
3 slices chicken roll	80
2 slices turkey roll	125

Fish	Calories
one serving broiled flounder	140
one serving broiled codfish	145
one serving broiled halibut	145
one broiled or baked salmon steak	205
3 ozs canned salmon	120
3 ozs canned tuna packed in water	127
or if packed in oil, well-drained	170
3 oz. canned crabmeat	85
4 breaded frozen fish sticks, heated in the oven	200
1 cup fresh cooked lobster	180
6-10 raw oysters (½ cup)	80
5-7 medium sardines, drained of oil and/or sauce	180
10 medium shrimp, boiled	100

Bread	Calories
1 slice rye	55
1 slice white	65
1 slice whole wheat toast	55
1 slice melba toast	17
1 bran muffin	125
1 corn muffin	155
1 plain muffin	135
1 baking powder biscuit	130
1 hard roll, medium size	160
2 soda crackers	45
2 rye wafers	45
2 saltines	35
2 bread sticks	50

Vegetables	Calories
1 cup asparagus (12 small spears)	40
1 cup green, snap, wax or yellow beans	30
1 cup beets	60
1 cup broccoli	40
1 cup brussels sprouts	40
1 cup cabbage	40
1 cup carrots	40
4 large (8-inch) stalks celery	20
1 cup collards	60
1 medium cucumber	25
6 ounces escarole, chicory, lettuce, watercress (salad basics)	30
1 cup kale	40
1 cup kohlrabi	50
½ cup canned mushrooms (not in butter or oil) or raw	15
6 small green onions	25
1 cup cooked or raw onion	60
1 cup peas	120

1 medium green pepper	15
4 small radishes	10
½ cup spinach	20
½ cup sauerkraut	15
1 cup winter squash	130
1 cup summer squash or zucchini	40
1 cup canned tomatoes	50
1 fresh medium tomato	30
1 cup turnips	40
1 cup eggplant	40

Fruits	*Calories*
one raw medium apple	70
½ cup unsweetened applesauce	40
3 fresh apricots	55
1 medium banana	85
½ cup fresh blueberries	45
½ cantaloupe	40
½ cup fresh cherries	50
½ grapefruit	50
½ cup purple grapes	50
½ cup green seedless grapes	50
1 medium orange	70
1 fresh peach	35
2 peach halves, canned in own juice	45
1 fresh small pear	100
2 pear halves, in own juice	100
2 slices pineapple raw or in own juice	40
1 fresh medium plum	30
3 stewed plums	90
½ cup fresh red raspberries	35
½ cup fresh strawberries	30
one medium tangerine	40
½ cup canned water packed fruit cocktail	40
3 ounces watermelon pulp	26

Juices	*Calories*
1 cup grapefruit juice	100
¾ cup orange juice	90
1 cup apple juice	125
1 cup cranberry juice cocktail	160
½ cup grape juice (diluted 1 to 3 with water)	75
½ cup pineapple juice	72
½ cup prune juice	120
1 cup tomato juice	48

Milk and Cheese	*Calories*
1 cup skim milk	90
1 cup buttermilk	85
½ cup uncreamed cottage cheese	110
1 ounce Camembert	85
2 tablespoons grated Parmesan	40
1 ounce ungrated Parmesan	130
½ cup plain yogurt	60

Potatoes, Pasta, Rice and Corn   *Calories*
(Serve from this exchange group a maximum of four times a week.)

1 potato medium, baked	100
¾ cup potatoes, mashed with skim milk	100
½ cup rice	94
½ cup cooked spaghetti	60
½ boiled sweet potato	85
½ cup macaroni	200
½ cup noodles	160
1 medium ear corn-on-cob	65
½ cup corn	85

Fixings	*Calories*
1 tablespoon mayonnaise	110
1 tablespoon oil and vinegar dressing	90

1 ounce no-calorie salad dressing	5
1 tablespoon corn oil	110
1 tablespoon corn oil margarine or butter	100
1 tablespoon honey	60
1 tablespoon peanut butter	90
1 cup beef or chicken bouillon	10
½ cup fruited flavored gelatin	80
2 jumbo green olives	15
2 jumbo black olives	15
1 large dill pickle	15
2 tablespoons catsup	30
2 tablespoons chili sauce	30

The Long Beach Project A Scale's Eye View

Child	Starting Weight	Final Weight	Weight Loss
1	91 1/2	81 1/4	10 1/4
2	73 3/4	68 1/2	5 1/4
3	114 1/2	112	2 1/2
4	58	55	3
5	91	87	4
6	105	95 3/4	4 1/4
7	105	100 1/2	5 1/2
8	56 1/4	53 3/4	2 1/2
9	74	69	5
10	92 1/2	89	3 1/2
11	132 1/4	130 3/4	1 1/2
12	100 1/4	94 1/2	5 1/4
13	66	64 1/2	1 1/2
14	100 1/2	98	2 1/2
15	98	97 1/2	1/2
16	133	123	10
17	131	122 3/4	8 1/4
18	145	140 1/2	4 1/4
19	104 1/2	103 1/4	1 1/2
20	110 1/2	107 1/2	3
21	70 2/4	68 1/4	2 1/2
22	110	107 1/2	2 1/2
23	102	97	5
24	160	154	6
			Weight Gain
25	161	164 1/4	3 1/4
26	66 1/2	67	1/2

Section II

THE AGES OF OVERTASTE

We call "The Ages of Overtaste" those times in a person's life when the Pleasure Economy is weakest and most susceptible to compensatory overtasting.

You can probably spot those times in your own life pretty easily. But if you are a parent, remember; as a feeder you are responsible for pleasure economies other than your own.

When we outline "The Ages of Overtaste" and ask you, "Which is your life?" we expect you to select all the lives in which you play a role.

The person, most likely the mother, who is responsible for the meals of other people, has to learn to identify with what is going on in the pleasure economy of her baby, her pre-adolescent and her teenager. She must understand what is happening in her own pleasure economy when she is pregnant; when she is a woman in her middle years and all her children are on their own; and when she has physical or emotional problems.

CHAPTER 4

Training the Young Taste Buds

The Pregnant Palate

Ever since we can remember, this great nation of rational people has held fast to the idea that pregnant women just naturally get crazy taste cravings.

We doctors have a funny feeling that many women give in to overtaste during pregnancy because tradition expects them to do so, not because they really want to. We know many women whose most outlandish dietary habit during pregnancy was that they sometimes got very hungry. And we know a lot of women who remember their pregnancies for what they didn't want to eat, not for what they had to stop eating. A "coffee freak" friend of ours could not bear to think of a cup of coffee when she was pregnant. She also gave up tea, cigarettes and liquor, because these items gave her terrible heartburn.

The morning after her baby was born, she sat up in bed, guzzled a cup of hospital coffee, borrowed a cigarette from an orderly and started all over again, with the passion of a long-lost lover. As far as her sense of taste and her eating habits were concerned, she was two different people during and after pregnancy.

Scientists call this distortion of normal taste patterns during pregnancy "pica."

The word really refers to any unusual craving to eat

something other than food. But this also refers to desires for foods that are regular food but which are not ordinarily liked by the eater. That is the kind of pica many pregnant women experience.

Pica occurs because pregnancy brings with it a vast change in a woman's body chemistry and an even greater change in her pleasure economy, with an accompanying new set of psychological stimuli for her sense of taste.

The problem if you are pregnant is this: how do you resist the temptation to overtaste at a time in your life when taste is one of your number one sensations?

Ask your doctor about the Long Beach Diet. Because this diet caters to so many different kinds of tastes, we believe its guidelines will adjust to whatever degree of pica you may experience. We believe that if you can eat according to the principles of the Long Beach Diet during pregnancy, you will have an easier time regaining your figure after pregnancy.

What the Tastefully Fed Infant Will Eat

While a woman is pregnant, she should be aware that her eating habits, her pleasure economy, will soon affect the life of another human being, her baby. If she has been eating unwisely up to now, she must change that pattern for the baby's sake. Remember, the palate of a newborn child is *tabula rasa*—a blank page waiting for her to write on it.

If she writes "whole milk with sugar added" or "sweetened orange juice" on that baby's palate, then she is building a taste for sugar. If she writes on that baby's palate, "fortified skim milk" or "unsweetened orange juice," she is building a taste for light, natural foods that do not contain excess sugar.

An infant gets gratification from eating in two ways: by sucking and by enjoying the feeling of a full stomach. His sense of taste is as yet a rather minor factor, in our opinion. It is his *mother's* sense of taste, the choices *she* makes for various foods—now in infancy; later, in early childhood; and even later, in middle age.

It is interesting to note that infants, left to their own devices, can choose nutritionally proper foods in reasonably correct amounts. Toward the end of the first year of life, the child's appetite alone assumes a key role in regulating food quantity. Studies conducted some fifty years ago by Dr. C.M. Davis of Chicago, point out that the appetite is a satisfactory guide, not only in regard to the quantity of food, but to the actual selection of food. Early in development, the body's needs alone dictate a nutritionally appropriate food intake via the appetite mechanism—taste operates only in the service of fulfilling body needs.

So, when a mother thinks about feeding her baby, she should use good judgment and not "think" with the often subconscious, sentimental and mistaken programming of her own sense of taste.

THE NINE RULES OF ENLIGHTENED FEEDING

The first rule of enlightened feeding: Mothers must learn to feed their children so that they grow better, not just bigger. The image of a plump child is commonly misinterpreted as a sign of robust health.

During the Vietnam War, the medical profession in this country was stunned by the results of autopsies on our casualties which revealed an alarming amount of advanced arteriosclerosis in our supposedly healthy, robust young soldiers. These boys were heading for early heart disease, high blood pressure and strokes.

It was this finding which awakened pediatricians to the problem of childhood nutrition. Because if these soldiers had hardening of the arteries at nineteen, they must have been acquiring hardening of the arteries since they were nine, or younger.

We pediatricians began taking a critical second look at the feeding practices of American parents. We made a number of observations. Some parents, for example, used chocolate additives in the whole milk of their children, in order to encourage them to drink more whole milk. Do these parents take the risk of making their children become unhealthy adults? We believe they do.

Some parents add eggs, a mistaken dietary supplement, to their children's whole milk and then disguise the eggnog with chocolate syrup. Those parents lay a shaky nutritional groundwork for future health.

It was not so long ago that children were encouraged to drink what parents thought was a hearty beef tea. This was made by taking a piece of top round, putting it in a strainer and mashing it into a cup of boiling water so that all the blood and the fat streamed out of it. The piece of meat was given to the cats. So the child got all the fat and watered down beef blood, while the cats got all the nutritious body building protein.

Some parents feed their children red meat seven or fourteen times a week. They are "larding" their children. Others adopt a *laissez-faire* attitude toward feeding, letting their children literally grow up on hot dogs, hamburgers and soda pop. They are aware of the potentially ill effects of additives on growing children.

Some parents allow their children to eat cream-filled packaged cakes twice a day, every day, for years and years. Those parents are making their children candidates for early diabetes.

110

And all of this terrible, ignorant feeding is done to "give our children the best!"

The second rule of enlightened feeding: Mother, if she is the feeder, must do her best to prevent overweight in her children now, so that it will not have to be corrected later on.

Here are some techniques of eating that we tell mothers to encourage at the table:

Teach them to chew long and savor the taste of each bite, to get more taste pleasure from small amounts of food. Most people who get fat from overtasting large quantities of food are doing so because they have somehow learned to undertaste each bite of food.

Do not permit children to wash down a mouthful of food with a liquid—they do not get any taste pleasure that way. That is how to take pills not how to eat. We believe people should put off drinking to the end of the meal.

Teach children to put down their utensils after every bite. It's surprising how this little habit will prolong each mouthful.

Foster conversation during mealtime, but not while chewing.

Allow no distractions such as television or interruptive telephone calls. If children eat while they are watching television, for example, they tend to forget that they have eaten and they still feel hungry when the show is over.

In an experiment by Drs. Hashim and Van Itallie of St. Luke's Hospital Center, New York, two groups of subjects, one obese, the other lean, were fed tasteless though fully nutritious food.

The food was offered in several ways, first through a feeding tube. The obese patient consumed only one tenth of the calories needed to maintain his weight—a drastic reduction. The lean subject ate just enough to maintain body weight.

To make the same food more attractive, they switched from an automatic feeding tube to a paper cup. The obese person consumed twice as much. The lean person was not affected.

The same formula was then placed in a crystal goblet. The obese person doubled his intake again. With a candle in the room, to create a more pleasurable dining atmostphere the obese person consumed even more. When told that the feeding machine had broken down, the subject was given regular food and ate even more. The lean person was still not affected.

Conclusions: The quantity of food consumed by the obese subject is increased by a variety of external factors. Doctors feel that these responses can be reconditioned.

We want to offer a few principles for mothers to keep in mind when they are planning the infant diet.

1. Babies prefer flavor to no flavor.

We are not sure how much taste discrimination babies have. But a couple of acts make us think they taste more than we ever expected.

The only thing that some babies do not like is water. We are training our mothers to make them like it. Why don't babies like water? Because it is not milk. However, if babies are given a choice between water and weak tea, we find that they will generally pick the tea. Why? Because babies prefer flavor to no flavor, they must therefore have a natural sense of taste.

This means that babies have the innate capacity to eat nourishing food, the milk instead of the water; to prefer the flavorful food, the tea instead of the water. And the flavor a baby chooses is not necessarily the sweet one.

2. The volume of food, not the taste, is what counts in appeasing a baby's hunger.

112

Babies prefer flavor; yes, but taste has little or nothing to do with their satisfaction with their food. The way we teach our babies to drink milk is a good case in point.

The best milk for the newborn is mother's milk. There is still nothing better on the market. However, we have to be realistic. Only five percent of our patients were actually breast fed by their mothers, so we recommend the prepared formulas that try to simulate breast milk. At three months, we prescribe skim milk for all our babies. They grow well and feel good on this milk. The right quantities satisfy the appetite. The flavor and texture and temperature of the milk are determined by us and the mother, and the baby is perfectly content to let us make these decisions.

This means that the mother of an infant has critical control over the tastes her baby will develop in later life. If she feeds her baby low-fat milk, he will be as satisfied as if she had fed him the same quantity of whole milk. And we believe the baby will be healthier in the long run, because his mother will be discouraging the formation of taste cravings for foods high in saturated fats.

3. A baby does not need excess salt to make its food tasty.

There is much evidence to show that when people add lots of extra salt to their food, they are contributing to the beginnings of hypertension, the medical term for high blood pressure.

Thanks to the concerted efforts of pediatricians, baby foods now have much lower concentrations of salt than in previous years. Baby foods formerly contained a higher amount of salt than breast milk. Cow's milk contains up to five times as much salt. Even if a mother is not breast feeding, it's still a good idea to use breast milk as nature's own best barometer of the proper salt, sugar, and calorie content for baby food.

At this time we do not really know what effect the salt in baby food will have in producing high blood pressure and hardening of the arteries before age forty-five. But we certainly know that infants (with their non-taste-controlled appetites) can do just as well with a lot less salt.

If a child is raised on a low salt diet, that child will continue to accept low salt intake as he grows older.

Remember, the taste created during infancy is the taste that will last a lifetime!

4. A mother can make her own baby food.

If a woman has any doubts at all about the baby food she plans to serve—if she thinks it has too much salt, too many calories, too much sugar—she can use the blender to make her own baby food.

Food is . . . whatever you want it to be. Home. Love. Pride—if the food is good and you did the cooking. History—if the food is traditional and your forefathers ate it. (Even sex—remember the eating scene in the movie version of *Tom Jones*?) In fact, food is probably a little bit of each of those things to all of us. When a mother is reorganizing the eating habits of her family, she has to keep that in mind.

People use food for all kinds of purposes. Some people eat so that they will not have to talk. Some people cannot sit down and talk seriously unless it is over a meal. Millions of people, in all societies, can find no better way to celebrate than by feasting. Remember how the Chinese deluged our ping-pong team with food at the onset of *detente* a few years ago?

If a man takes a woman to dinner, he is considered to be more serious about her than if he takes her to a ball game.

Holidays all over the world, in all religions, are commemorated by whether one fasts or feasts. Either way the emphasis is on eating.

Why all these complicated "hangups" about food?

It starts when you are a baby. Feeding is your first relationship. Your first love affair was with the hand that fed you when you were an infant.

If the hand that fed you fed you on time and with real love, then you have a pretty good chance of growing up without too many hangups about food. We tell our mothers to cuddle their babies while they are eating; to hold their babies close to their breasts; to talk to their babies during meals. We advise them to breast-feed their babies if they possibly can. If they do not feed their babies that way—if they prop them in a chair, stick a bottle in their mouths, let them eat alone in silence, untouched without talking to them, food could become one of their big problems later in life. A child or adult may want more and more of it, the way he wanted more of his mother's love and attention. Every time something goes wrong, he may find himself gobbling boxes of cookies to restore his sense of affection and security.

The grown-up baby may find himself feeling that the more food he eats, the more love he is getting. And even worse, that the more food a mother feeds, the more love she is giving.

We have a particular patient who is very fat. Her mother was called and asked what the child had been eating. It turned out that this mother, who was born in Europe, was giving her little girl great quantities of candy on demand.

"In Europe," she said, "when I was growing up, candy was a luxury; it was very expensive. My brother and I almost never tasted candy. In America, it is cheap and plentiful. I cannot resist giving my child this pleasure."

We practice a little psychology, like most other physicians. We sympathized with that mother's need to stuff her little girl full of chocolate. But we will not condone it!

There is no point for a mother to ruin a child's life in an effort to pay herself back for her own childhood deprivations. That mother has to be stopped!

If you are such a mother, do not wait for a doctor to call you into his office before you begin to analyze your own psychology as far as food is concerned. Stand back and watch yourself eating, watch yourself feeding for a week and try to figure out what food really means to you. Try to figure out if you are overfeeding and/or overtasting for any good reason at all.

The man with the best insight into the power of food over the subconscious mind was the famous French novelist Marcel Proust whose mother baked delicious cookies.

All Proust had to do was to smell those cookies, and he remembered everything his mother had ever done or said: he remembered everything he had ever felt about her; he remembered their house, her clothes, their evenings and afternoons. He remembered years and years of events he might never have recalled, had it not been for the smell of her cookies.

Most of us can find an example of how we associated food with remembrances of good times past. If the food was non-nutritious and the times were good, we are likely to return to that food every time we want to recapture the feel of those times again.

If you are Italian and you loved your mother, she probably fed you pasta with rich, home-made tomato sauce. No doubt you associate pasta with love and you are likely to love pasta.

If you are Chinese and you loved your mother, and she probably fed you fried rice with every meal. Undoubtedly, you associate fried rice with love and you are likely to love fried rice.

Now, there is not a thing wrong with pasta, or with fried rice, for that matter if it is eaten no more than twice a week. We would not ask anyone to give up the beloved symbols of his or her ethnic heritage. We are saying that it will not make you more Italian to overtaste pasta, nor will it make you more Chinese to overtaste fried rice. The person who eats ten *blinchiki* will not be more Russian than the one who eats two—he will only be fatter.

So we say to mothers, "Let your children remember your dinners for the good conversation, for being together, not for the overly rich desserts."

Follow the rules for enlightened feeding that we set forth in the following pages. Let your children remember your loving care whenever they taste fresh fruit or yogurt. Then in 2001, when your children are flying to Mars on the space shuttle, they may just serve meals in the new great American tradition of sensible eating, enjoying their nostalgia without getting too fat to enjoy weightlessness!

If a mother wishes to prevent her child from becoming part of the terrifying health statistics for overweight adults, she must feed the right food during the formative years of her child's life. There are three reasons.

First, these are the years when a child learns how to eat.

Second, these are the years when a child's basic taste preferences are formed. And the taste habits of the child are the key to the eating habits of the adult.

Third, these are the years when the basic cell structure of the body is determined, when the body creates, through the child's eating patterns, the number of fat storage cells it should and will have for the rest of his life.

Dr. Jerome Knittle, an expert on obesity in children, described his study in the *Journal of Pediatrics,* December 1972,* which confirmed scientifically what we have been observing in our practice for years. Children who are not fat, Knittle says, have cell-sizes below those of adults. These cells stay below adult size well into the eleventh year.

Children who are fat, Dr. Knittle says, have more fat cells than non-obese children. In his study, Dr. Knittle found that the fat cells had reached adult size in many overweight children while they were in the sixth to eleventh year.

We think mothers will be surprised how much a slow, leisurely, conversation-filled meal will do to recapture the feeling of family that has been so shattered in our society.

We tell mothers not to keep fattening foods around to tempt children. We stock our office with fruit.

One day, when we first started our practice together, I watched Henry Lichter eat an apple. First, Henry cut the apple in half. He ate one half in one bite. Then he gulped the other half in one bite. The whole apple was gone in a matter of seconds.

I asked Henry how the apple tasted. Henry did not know. He had derived absolutely no taste pleasure income from that apple because he had eaten it too quickly. No wonder his palate told him he was hungry again in an hour.

*Jerome L. Knittle, M.D. "Obesity in Childhood? A problem in Adipose Tissue Cellular Development." *Journal of Pediatrics,* December 1972. Vol. 81 No. 6, p. 1048.

Today, Henry the Enlightened Eater has learned the technique of slicing apples very, very thinly and eating one slice at a time. If Henry can learn to eat that way, you too can learn to eat—and feed—that way.

The third rule of enlightened feeding: A parent should not make it harder for a child to be thin by being fat themselves.

If one parent is fat, then the children have a 40 to 50 percent chance of being fat themselves. If both parents are fat, the children have a 70 to 80 percent chance of being obese.

Your three-year-old daughter may be pleasingly plump now, but are the odds stacked against her in such a way that she will be miserable in high school? Are you programming your children to be fat? Remember, the parent who is fat can be the father or the mother. If you have not been worrying about your husband's thirty or forty extra pounds for his sake, at least worry about it for the children's sake. Do not be egotistical. Your fat is not the only important fat in the family.

Just in case you were blaming your obesity on your family inheritance, remember this. Important studies have shown that 'hereditary', obesity and 'acquired' obesity in children are equally responsive to a program of weight reduction based upon reduced caloric intake."* That means you can be slim just as easily as if you had slim parents. If mama was skinny, you can be skinny—if mama was rotund, you can be skinny!

We are presenting the percentages for offspring of fat parents because we want you to know you are making it

*Platon Collipp, Beneard Schmierer, Joseph Greensher, Iraj Rexvani and Michael Halle. "Childhood Obesity—To Treat or Not to Treat." *Medical Times,* March 1971. Vol. 99, No. 3, p. 155.

harder for your child if you are fat. You are not making it impossible, any more than your overweight parent made it impossible for you.

The fourth rule of enlightened feeding: Exercise should be as natural a part of daily life as eating.

Overweight children tend to be underactive. In fact, they are often trapped in a vicious circle. As they put on weight, they become less physically active, and the less active they are, the more likely they are to put on additional weight.

Observations of babies in cribs reveal that fat infants are less active than slender ones. And observations of children watching television are similarly revealing. Overweight youngsters, sit in front of the set "hardly moving a muscle, for half an hour or more on end." Curiously, they are almost as expressionless as they are motionless.

We have seen films of obese children at play. When they swim, they do so lazily, even lethargically; their arms and legs do not propel them as they do in the case of the other children. When overweight children play tennis, they hit the ball when it comes to them but they do not run to get a ball that has been hit out of their reach.

So when the mother of a fat child comes into the office and says, "But, Doctor, he is so active!" We know. And she should know too, that her child is nowhere as active as he ought to be.

There is, however, a bright side. As obesity disappears, physical activity will usually increase spontaneously.

It should also go without saying, but unfortunately needs to be said emphatically: that what is true for the child is equally true for the adult. Exercise should be as natural a part of life as eating. The trouble is that we tend to think of exercise in terms of engaging in a sport or doing calisthenics. We have forgotten that exercise is a matter of exerting ourselves in the normal course of the day.

Walking up the stairs instead of taking an elevator or escalator is exercise. Walking briskly instead of taking the car is exercise. So is bicycling, ice-skating or jogging. If you think that you are too old to do such things, think what you are really saying about yourself: you are describing yourself as old.

There is no need for us to point out that such sports as tennis, golf, swimming or skiing are effective exercise. But it seems worth mentioning that exercise alone will not cause permanent weight loss. The purpose of exercise, as far as weight control is concerned, is to help use up the calories that we inevitably gain in a normal day's eating and, even more important, to keep our bodies limber and trim.

The energy value of food is measured in calories—units of heat energy. The amount of calories or energy a person needs depends on his or her weight and the amount of daily muscular activity. We need about a calorie a minute just to stay alive, and the rest of our energy needs are determined by our physical activities.

A regular period of activity, on a daily basis, should accompany your new diet. Be as strict about it as you are about following your diet. Try to make your daily routine a little more strenuous—walk instead of driving, or better yet, jog! As a caloric guide to taking off weight in an exercise program, the following should be kept in mind:

Calories Consumed per minute

Resting in bed	1.2
Walking upstairs	20.0
Playing football	10.1

Whatever your activity, make sure you do it regularly. It's a valuable aid to your diet program and it will help your disposition.

Your Personal Calorie Meter

A person who weighs about 150 pounds and is moderately active requires 15 calories for each pound of body weight, or a total of 2250 calories a day to maintain his present body weight. The amount of calories consumed must balance with the daily energy requirements of the body. All of the calories we eat over and above this total are stored as fat, and too many excess calories lead to excess weight.

If you weigh 150 pounds and want to lose weight, say a pound a week, you must reduce your daily caloric intake by 500 calories, from 2250 to 1750 calories a day. To lose two pounds a week, reduce your daily caloric intake by 1200—from 2250 to 1250 per day.

Present Weight	Present Daily Intake (to maintain present weight)	Daily Caloric Intake to lose 1 lb. a week 600 calories less	Daily Caloric Intake to lose 2 lbs. a week 1200 calories less
150 pounds	2250	1750	1250
200 pounds	3000	2500	2000
250 pounds	3750	3250	2750

Keeping in shape is physically desirable. It is also psychologically desirable. The better we feel about ourselves, the easier it is to eat wisely and control our weight. Since this book has been designed to focus on the nutritional principles that regulate weight control, it cannot deal at any length with the part that exercise plays. But this point must be emphasized: *From the beginning to the end of this book, it is assumed that you are using your body as well as your brain in gaining control of your weight.*

Physical activity alone will not make a child slim any more than simply working out at the gym will take the pounds off an adult. But physical activity will make a child stronger. It will put added pressure on his metabolic system to burn up stored fat.

As for sports, these have too long been thought of as necessary primarily for boys. This notion is being challenged in our era, and we think none too soon. Girls must be healthy too. If a mother has a tomboy, perhaps she should consider herself lucky. So just as she would pick out a musical instrument for her girl or boy to learn, we recommend that she pick out a sport for her children—and make it a sport that moves the body!

The fifth rule of enlightened feeding: Parents should not make life too easy for their children.

We believe that many parents with the very best intentions make life unhealthfully inactive for their children. Now that the household workload has been simplified by gadgetry so that one person can handle it all, the children are not required to do as much in the home. That is a piece of "progress" we could all probably live without. From a psychological point of view, it has probably weakened the family. And from a health point of view, it has decreased the activity of children.

123

So if you're a mother, next time you are scrubbing the floor, try sharing the caloric expenditure with your eight-year-old. For him, it might be fun.

In addition, we believe that American parents chauffeur their children too much. Not only is the pollution from the car's exhaust bad for the air—which makes the air unhealthy for everybody—but children are also being driven places where they could just as well walk. Bicycles are too often used as toys alone and not enough as transportation. So we suggest that mothers rethink their car pooling route. Could the child walk to Sunday school? Can a child walk to the park? Could he take his bike to his friend's house? We say to mothers:"Do not think so much of your child's comfort; think more of his muscles."

Remember, the correlation between inactivity and weight gain is undeniable. When farmers want to fatten their livestock, they pen them up.

The sixth rule of enlightened feeding: Set limits on television watching—when and how much.

Too much of the food advertising beamed at children and at mothers is clearly counter-nutritional. There are a number of products urged upon children which do not fall anywhere within the guidelines of the Long Beach Diet, and which the prudent parent would be wise to include on a "Household Hate Parade of Forbidden Foods." If a mother tunes out only the advertising for sugared foods, she will be helping to save her child from the risk of degenerative diseases associated with high sugar intake, from diabetes and coronary thrombosis to gallstones and cancer.

The battle against counter-nutritional advertising is being fought endlessly in the courts, before congressional committees, in medical journals and newspapers.

124

New natural unsweetened cereals being offered today are a different product of the food industry's desire to satisfy critics of those sugared, colored, processed cereals said to have too little nutritional value. (In one famous experiment, scientists fed one group of newborn rats a popular breakfast cereal and milk and fed another group milk with shredded cardboard. The two groups grew at exactly the same rate!)

If you're a parent, be aware of the danger; be aware of the debate. Do not wait for the Surgeon General to label supersweet, cream-filled snacks as possibly "dangerous to your health." Label them now, with your own seal of disapproval.

There is another way to fight counter-nutritional television advertising.

Do what Dr. Pisacano did with his six children. Turn off the TV set, stand in front of it and announce, "Here is your father! Live! In living color!"

And talk to them.

The seventh rule of enlightened feeding: Mothers can be aware of their own bad taste habits and should try to avoid transmitting them to their children.

We know you enjoy your traditional breakfast cereal which you ate during your formative years. Your taste buds are conditioned to it. Maybe you even associate it with warm, homey breakfast table memories. Furthermore, you may not even be able to imagine eating or serving any other kind of cereal.

But think for a minute—does your child have that same hangup? Just because those natural cereals they are selling now taste strange to you, there is no reason why your four-year-old will not love them. Just buy some, put it in a bowl and pour skim milk on it; do not add sugar; if you wish add a sliced banana or some fresh berries.

Keep your own mis-trained sense of taste to yourself and your child will probably enjoy that cereal. If you learn to follow this seventh rule, you will allow your child to develop his or her own taste preferences for nutritious food, independent of your mistaken taste habits.

The eighth rule of enlightened feeding: Vitamins are not in themselves good nutrition.

Vitamins are abundant in the average American balanced diet, and vitamin additives are generally not needed by normal children. In some advertising, vitamins are proposed as a substitute for good eating.

If a child does not eat well, vitamin therapy is not the easy answer. With a youngster who will not eat green vegetables, we suggest that a mother not count on vitamins to fill the nutritional needs those vegetables should fill.

Do not forget that the key to a child's lifelong eating habits lies in a sense of *taste*. By giving the child a tasteless (or worse, sweetened) vitamin pill instead of string beans, a mother encourages her youngster to give up the taste of string beans, developing no tolerance or attachment for it.

If she cannot get the child to eat string beans, we recommend broccoli, or other greens. Or peas, brussels sprouts, spinach, kale, turnips, carrots—vegetables *she* has never eaten. Many children will relish raw vegetables which they will not eat cooked. (Celery sticks, for instance.) Stand back. Let the child eat according to his own natural sense of taste.

The ninth rule of enlightened feeding: Always read the list of ingredients. (The first ingredient is the major ingredient.)

If the fruit punch contains at least ten or even twenty percent real fruit juice, think more about the other eighty to ninety percent. If it tastes like sugar and water, then do not drink it. It may contain great-sounding recommended daily requirements of all kinds of vitamins, but it may also contain too much sugar for a child to consume.

The mother of one of our overweight patients asked recently, "But what shall I do with all those cookies, all those cream-filled little cakes, all that sugar-coated cereal? I cannot just throw them out."

"Why not?"

"Because . . . because . . . because . . . I just can't!" she cried. "It is food! You cannot waste food!"

"It is not food," John answered. "It is less nutritious than potato peelings and fish bones, and you throw them out all the time." (The average calories in one cream-filled cookie per day in excess of your needs will put on one extra pound of weight every year!)

So our mother went home . . . and she gritted her teeth and threw it out. All of it. Later when she passed it in the aisles of the supermarket, she shut her eyes and her mind and did not buy.

It takes as much will power not to feed as it does not to eat. Just remember, you are "not feeding" to save your children!

CHAPTER 5

The Riddle of the Fat Teenager

When my son was a freshman in high scool, he came to me for some advice on a term paper. He had been assigned to write an explanation of the opening sentence in Dickens' *A Tale of Two Cities:* "It was the best of times; it was the worst of times."

I looked at him, with his just-changed voice still occasionally squeaking, with his pimples, his splotchy young beard, his nervous tension, his awful shyness, his wild exaltations and raucous laughter, and I thought, you are it, son.

Adolescence is the best of times; it is the worst of times. If we could all be immunized against the tricks of fate and could live in a state of constant pleasure, most of us would probably hate adolescence but look upon it as the best and the worst time in our lives.

The adolescent is under terrible pressure. His body is changing and startling him. His mind is playing weird, diabolical tricks on him. What a fantasy life he has! We should all be so interested in our daydreams.

He anguishes. He makes resolutions and breaks them immediately. He thinks his parents are crazy and mysterious. One high-school girl told us that she feared her forty-year-old mother was becoming senile. "I am really worried about her," she said. "Can't they give her something to calm her down?" When this girl is twenty-one, she will probably be amazed at how much her mother has learned in four or five years!

So stirred up is the teenager by all this tumult within and without, that traditionally he seeks the solace of faddism and ferocious solidarity among his own ranks. Sameness is his shelter. The worst thing that can happen to an adolescent, in his own opinion, is that he should be different from all the other adolescents in town.

A fat adolescent girl can dress the same as her peers. Her gorgeous hair may gleam as brightly and blow as romantically as that of any other teenager. But if she is fat, she is different. The one great comfort of this trying time of life, which is to be the same as everybody else, is denied her. The extra load on her body is far outweighed by the extra load on her mind. Far more of our teenage patients cry in our office because they are fat then do our toddler patients because we have given them an injection.

Young people start feeling self-conscious about their excess weight during the pre-adolescent years, when self-awareness begins to take over. Suzanne Levine, now a sleek, slim New York magazine editor, was a fat child. She recalls every detail of her pre-adolescent and adolescent overweight. The scars are there forever, no matter how sleek and slim she had become as an adult:

> I was about nine the first time I really noticed my size getting in the way. A bunch of us were horsing around in the schoolyard, when we decided to invade the "little kids" playground and take a ride on their swings—those little box-like affairs that look like half a high chair. My friends . . . squirmed into the cramped little seats while I struggled to wedge in first one buttock and then the other. Finally, in humiliated despair, I fled. And as the saying goes, I

129

never stopped running (home to the icebox for solace).*

The pre-adolescent years lie between the time when it was easy to eat nutritious, slimming foods, and the time when it becomes terribly hard to change tasting habits. Those are the years when a child become self-conscious, when he starts to open the refrigerator on his own—when his mother is no longer the only control. And the first time he hears somebody yell out, "Hey, Fatso. . . ." He retreats to the refrigerator for solace, compensating himself with excess taste pleasure.

We believe there are at least two kinds of pre-adolescent overweight. The first is a direct result of bad eating habits in early childhood, resulting in excess fat storage deposits. The second is possibly just a side effect of the onset of puberty. This second kind of pre-adolescent overweight does not seem worrisome to us if the child's tasting habits and physical examination are normal. Conditions even out in the next few years, and if the child has been eating properly, then a permanent overweight problem is not likely to develop.

If you are a mother dealing with a teenage girl with a diet problem, try to remember when she became fat. If it was before nine or ten years of age, then you must tackle the problem of overtaste and tackle it now, vigorously. If she began being pudgy just at the onset of puberty and her eating habits are good, then take it easy, and do not pressure her to diet. As she grows to womanhood, the extra weight may very well be redistributed just the way she wants it to be. What we are concerned with in this chapter is the fat teenager who became that

*Suzanne Levine, "Confessions of a Formerly Fat Girl," *Cosmopolitan Magazine.* October 1971, p.98. (Copyright 1971 The Hearst Corporation. All rights reserved.)

way because of bad tasting habits, both inside and out-side the home.

Why Is It So Hard for Teens to Diet?

The first thing a parent must find out is why the child has an overweight problem.

Is the source of the overweight metabolic? Is it from a malfunction in the endocrine system? (Incidentally, thyroid disorders are very rarely a cause of overweight in children who are otherwise normal.) Is it a psycholog-ical problem requiring counseling and special attitudinal responses from the parent? Or is it just a result of ter-rible tasting habits?

Once a physical examination has proven to the parent and the child that there is no organic cause for the overweight, then both of them have to sit down and analyze the objective factors that may be contributing to the condition.

We already have admitted that teenagers are under terrible pressure. In this atmosphere of tension, the last thing that a teenager can do is deprive himself of the very thing he relies on to relive the tension—the extra taste pleasure he gets from food.

A second contributory factor is self-hatred of the fat teenager. Such children loathe their bodies, wanting more than anything else in the world to be slim and to be accepted by their peer group. They demean them-selves. The more they hate themselves, the more they eat to punish themselves for being fat. Studies of over-weight teenagers have shown that these children are ter-ribly preoccupied with weight, that they rate people by whether they are slim or fat (the slim ones are terrific, the fat ones are horrible) and that they blame all their failures in life on being fat. Every time the mother of such a child, nags a child not to eat, or even mentions weight, salt is poured on an open wound, adding to the child's sense of inferiority. We have had mothers come into our offices, distraught and feeling helpless, because they simply could not reason with a fat teenage child about dieting. "The minute I mention diet, Doctor," said one mother, "she looks at me like she hates me, or she cries."

But remember, it is not the parent she hates—it is herself.

However helpless a mother may feel, she must not—dare not—stop coping.

We believe that one way to relieve the crisis of discussing diet with an overweight teenager is not to talk about it at all—but do something. Keep the fattening foods out of the house. Do not hide them from them—they will find them. If the mother is hiding food in order to give it to her husband, we urge mothers not to do that, either. A husband can do without such foods. We recommend that mothers fill their refrigerators with carrot sticks and skim milk cheese; we tell them to fill their pantry full of whole grain crackers and tuna fish packed in water . . . no oil. We urge them to take up jogging and take the child along. Perhaps, if a mother jogs too, the child will not feel peculiar doing it herself.

And when a daughter cannot find any clothes to fit except a size 18 dress, we tell this mother not to tell the saleslady how awful it is that their daughter is so fat! Keep the pressure off! Of all the Ages of Overtaste, the adolescent years is the time when parents have to give their children a low-profile diet, and lots of emotional support.

One last factor complicates the adolescent diet, which is the monumental amount of non-nutritious food served to and consumed by children during their high school years. When Sophie Portnoy, the much maligned mother in Philip Roth's novel *Portnoy's Complaint,* hollered at her son for eating at "Caesar's Chaserai Palace," she was right on target. "Chaserai" is a Yiddish word meaning "garbage" or "pig food." Whatever Mrs. Portnoy meant, we know what we mean—endless bottles of sweetened soda pop, high in sugar, low in nutrition; endless hot dogs and hamburgers; starchy meals served in teenage hangouts and from food stands at football games and in the school cafeteria. All of these foods are high in fat (in the case of most hot dogs), colorings and additives that may be dangerous for the future health of the child—endless snacks from machines and tons of cookies, popcorn and candy bars consumed unthinkingly in the darkness of movie theatres.

A teenager is no longer a baby. He or she knows something about how the human body works. We advise parents to give their teenagers a copy of the Long Beach Diet suggesting they read it together to get those basic principles into their collective minds. If a mother rigidly changes the taste habits in the home, her child may recognize the importance of nutritional habits and continue the pattern on his own outside the home.

What a Concerned Parent and Concerned Teen Can Do

Let us reason together about pre-adolescent diets. There is much that mothers, as feeders and counselors, can do to help their children. There is a lot that the overweight teenager can do to help himself.

Karen B. had a typical adolescent dieting pattern:

"Like many run-of-the-mill fat teenagers," she wrote, "I tried everything from crash diets to self-hypnosis to lose weight. At age fifteen when I discovered I had gained weight, I immediately started starving myself.

After three weeks of little food, and little energy, I had lost a lot of weight. That might have been the end of my problem, had I returned to sensible eating. But I did not. I wanted food, food and more food. I gained much more than I had lost. If I was not eating, I was very depressed about my situation but just unaware of what to do about it."

Luckily for Karen, she realized that her fantasies of instant skinniness would never work in the real world. She began to follow the guidelines of the Long Beach Diet. "I am still battling my weight," she wrote, "and I am going to get candy medication for weight control to give me that little push. I do not expect to miraculously lose weight from medicated chewing gum or candy, my outlook on miracles has changed. However, I expect to refrain from filling up on goodies and I am going to stick to the recommended diet."

Her maximum weight was 165 pounds. Now she has almost reduced to her weight goal of 115 pounds.

The factor that enabled Karen to lose weight was her development of a mature attitude toward dieting. One of the feeders in a home must have that—either the mother or the child. Like Karen, somebody in the house had to stop believing in dieting miracles. Karen had been dieting with the same style in which she had been overeating. Taste, taste, and more taste—starve, starve, and more starvation. Adolescents are by their very nature extremists of mood and Karen was no different. As soon as she could even imagine moderation, she stopped needing instant gratification for her desires to be thin and she began to think of her overweight problem in the perspective of a lifetime.

Teenage Fat: The Defense Mechanism

Being fat is one of the best "cop-outs" in the world. If you are fat, you probably cannot compete athletically or socially. If you do not have to cope you do not take the risk of losing.

Suzanne Levine recalled how she, as a fat teenager, made copping out into a fine art.

> I would be anyone's friend and confidante, and had an active—if vicarious—social life. I spent many a Monday advising the boys whom to ask out, then Tuesday reassuring the girls that they *would* be asked, the rest of the week planning their wardrobe and date strategy, and Saturday night alone with "Gunsmoke." This is not to say I was not popular. *Listen, I made no demands on my male friends and was no threat to my girl friends.* [Our Italics.] I was very popular . . . that is, I was invited to parties—and I gave parties—but I was rarely asked to dance. Yes, I did go on diets—I would start a new one practically every week, *but my motivations were sadly weakened by the thought that if I did get skinny, I would have to compete with the other girls in the clothes-boy-dating game . . . a thought that was terrifying because I did not know how.* [Also our italics.]

Here is another great danger. Once a teenager is fat, he or she learns how to live with it. A certain kind of trust comes to those who are overweight—nobody has any reasons to feel jealous or threatened. That can get to be sort of fun after a while. At least a person can grow dangerously accustomed to it. We say "dangerously," because if one likes the role of "harmless lump" too much, the fat person may not only never get slim but he may never learn to compete either.

We know a boy very interested in music who was an

*Levine, *op. cit.*, p. 98.

excellent pianist,.wanting nothing better than to practice five or six hours a day. The other children made fun of him. They called him Eggy (short for Egghead). He had no interest in sports or clothes. The girls in his school sometimes looked interesting to him, but he was shy and afraid to approach them. Instead he ate a little something extra to comfort himself.

By the time he weighed 185 pounds (he was rather short), nobody cared if he practiced ten or twelve hours a day. They called him Fatso and let him be an egghead in peace. He did not have to overcome his shyness with girls because they would not go out with him anyway. He did not have to apologize to anyone (including himself) for not being able to throw a basketball into a basket because he simply was not a likely prospect for the team.

What this boy's parents failed to tell him was that you do not play basketball in order to make the team. You play basketball to give your muscles something to do!

Later on in life, when he was attending a very prominent music conservatory, surrounded as he was by other young people who shared his interests and valued his talent, he found the motivation to diet. He simply did not have the strength during his adolescence to wrestle with all the complicated problems of adjusting in a relatively hostile high school society in which he was so different intellectually that it made life easier if he was different physically, too. At the conservatory, he was equal intellectually. He wanted to compete with the other members of the orchestra the way he had never wanted to compete with the boys on the basketball team. So he lost weight. In effect, he had saved himself for a better time.

Because of this episode, no one should assume that it is permissible to wait until he is grown up to lose weight—absolutely not.

Our talented musician wasted the golden years of opportunity. He became an adult without developing the natural strength of his muscles, not caring for his body. He will never feel altogether good about his appearance. He became an adult without developing his body's natural talent at using stored fat for energy. Now that he is an adult, his fat storage cells, are large and numerous and accustomed to being unused. Now when he diets, as he always must, he is at war with his metabolism.

If you correct your eating habits when you are young, you may develop a metabolism that is friendly to your figure and keeping weight off will not be a struggle for the rest of your life.

How Lillian L. and Edward M. Learned to Control Their Taste and Their Weight

Edward M. of Ohio weighed 250 pounds in 1971 at the age of fifteen.

"I always wanted to lose weight. But I figured, when the girls came around to my friends, I said to myself, 'You are fat, they will not go out with you. So why diet?'

"When I finally decided to go on a diet (I figured it would not last), I went over to the store for my sister, noticed candy medication for weight control on display and bought a box. The turning point in my life came that night after supper. I would usually have a bowl of ice cream with pie and milk. That was only the beginning. Then I would have maybe a glass of chocolate milk, some cookies, a bottle of pop, some chips. But that night, I had a couple of the candies with a bottle of diet pop and did not eat another thing.

"I figured, this cannot last long. But it was still going on four weeks later. When I stepped on the scale, I saw that I had lost five pounds!"

At age seventeen, Edward weighed 185 pounds. He is now 6'1" tall and he still watches his weight. ("I know what it is like to be fat and I never want to be that way ever again.") His extra poundage had come off slowly taking him a year and a half to reach 185 pounds, a loss of 65 pounds. However, he was mature enough to understand that dieting does not have to be fast to be satisfying. The important thing is to develop a lasting reorganization of eating habits.

Edward no longer needs the pie, the milk, the cookies and the potato chips after dinner. He has re-trained his sense of taste so that he can get the same amount of sensual pleasure from less food and from less fattening foods. Of course, he is getting additional gratification now. "Believe it or not, the girls are asking me for dates!" he declares with enthusiasm.

Remember this if you are a teen or the parent of a dieting teen: if you are not gaining weight you are losing it. Adolescents are still growing. If you can maintain your weight, you will be able to count on its redistribution. For example: if you are five feet two inches tall and weigh 150 pounds, you are fat. But when you get to be five feet eight inches in height and still weigh 150, you will not be so fat anymore.

Mrs. L. from Washington was a fat teenager and did not lose weight until after her first child was born. She still has not reduced to her proper weight but she diets almost all the time. The legacy of her adolescence is still with her and it has taken years for her to find the motivation to really reorganize her eating habits, to re-train her sense of taste and thereby curb her appetite. Her advice to teenagers was: lose it while you are young.

"Sit down and think," said Lillian, "about what your life is going to be like, being fat forever. Sit down with your parents and ask them to help you diet. My mom would always do a lot of baking and one time when I lost fourteen pounds, she got real mad at me because she said I was losing my health. She got me so nervous and upset that I gained it all back.

"You have to sit down with your folks and tell them how much it means to you to lose weight. The first thing I worried about when I had my little girl was her weight. I was teased about it when I was younger; I was called Fatso. I certainly did not want her to have to go through that. You have to constantly think slim. Take a picture from a magazine of some beautiful woman who has a terrific slim figure and put it on the refrigerator. Every time you go to open the door, she will be there, staring at you, telling you, 'Hey, Fatso, don't you want to look like me?' That makes it a lot harder to go ahead and open the refrigerator."

Lillian L's fat adolescence was probably worth the agony just because of what it is now doing for her little girl. That little girl "eats smart." She is not going to be surprised at age thirteen by the fact that she weighs 180 pounds. Fortunately that little girl has a mother who knows the value of organizing a sensible taste/pleasure economy in childhood, before being fat becomes a lifelong problem.

We want all little girls and boys to be that lucky.

CHAPTER 6

The Kitchen, the Kids, and "Keeping Weight Off"

We have pretty much covered other lives—your children's, your husband's —the lives of the great multitude who are the American "fed "—and your life as a "feeder."

Now let us discuss your life as an "eater"—a grown-up, decently informed, responsible, sensible, tasteful eater.

When a young woman leaves home, she is almost always making a basic change in her pleasure economy. She may be going to work, living in her own apartment, sharing an apartment with other young women; she may be going to college or trade school. Either way, she must meet new standards and pass new tests all the time. In the motherless privacy of her new life, she makes all kinds of basic decisions about her appearance that are likely to stay with her forever.

We have had many patients who returned when they were grown to tell us that as soon as they were out on their own, they somehow "miraculously" started to lose weight. With our fat boy musical genius, life at the conservatory changed his habits and he did not have to hide his personality behind a wall of fat any more. For one girl, just having her own kitchen altered her life. All of a sudden, the grocery money came out of her own pocket; the trips to the supermarket came out of her own time. She was so busy living her own life that she just did not have time to eat so much.

All of us know girls who started losing weight the minute they fell in love. He was the necessary motivation—he was a "natural amphetamine" and probably had just as powerful an effect on body chemistry. People in love are hardly ever hungry because the desire to overtaste—brought on by a deficiency in the pleasure economy disappeared when that deficit was covered by a new pleasure, the best pleasure of all—love.

We do not worry too much about young women who go out on their own, who stock their own refrigerators with money budgeted from their own salaries, who make their own curfews and choose their own recreation.

We are concerned more with the young woman who settles down to marry, to keep house and raise children.

If you were fat when you were first married, then maybe the first flush of love will encourage you to remain as slim as a gymnast. After all, you do not have any reason to hate yourself or feel lonely any more, the way you may have when you were in high school. The man you married obviously loves you, no matter how much there is of you. Maybe you will begin fulfilling the image he has of you by getting slim and actually becoming as beautiful as he thinks you are.

We know women for whom marriage balanced the pleasure deficit they had been feeling all during those awful adolescent years. They no longer had to seek compensatory sensual gratification through overtaste. There was nothing to compensate for—life was terrific now.

But the exact opposite can happen as well, whether you were fat or sylphlike as an adolescent.

In some instances, women begin "compensatory overtasting" after marriage. Sometimes the marriage may not be working and there is a clear source of deficiency in

141

their pleasure economy. One way to make an unstable marriage worse is to become fat and unattractive. Then you will fulfill the present image your husband has of you—you will look as awful as he thinks you are.

We know a number of women who are pretty fat and pretty unhappy in their marriages. They overtaste because they are miserable. But when a friendly doctor says, "Why don't you make a trial separation?" they answer, "How can I leave? What man would look at a big fat woman like me?" So they stay, and remain miserable.

You see, there are many different graves to dig by overtasting. Very often, however, there is nothing obviously wrong with the marriage at all, and still the wife gets fat. Why?

When we were boys, it was pretty much accepted that women could get fat with impunity once they were married. It accompanied the married state; it went with producing children. Since everybody expected you to lose your figure after you had children, you did.

Today's woman is different. Married women want to be as slim and attractive as single career women on the covers of the fashion magazines. But, why do they still get fat in so many cases?

Homemaking is one of the most difficult jobs in the world. In our view, the average American mother who comes into a pediatrician's office with her children is a moderately depressed, chronically fatigued prisoner of her station in life. For years, we have seen pretty, sweet-tempered women trudge into our offices, worn out from rushing to make their appointments on time, trying to keep their children out of trouble in the waiting room, snapping irritably or whining wearily. And all these years we have wanted to say to them, "Lady, you need a booster more than your child does. You need somebody to put clean sheets on your bed and bring you chicken

142

soup and tell you stories, and advise you to go to sleep for a week."

Lately, more and more people have begun to realize that unfair burdens are placed on women. The solution most frequently offered in ads, and the one we hate the most is that "the worn-out mother" should not cook tonight. Instead they advise you to take your family out for a fast-food dinner consisting of a number of pre-fried, pre-cooked or pre-mixed "delights" that are terrible for everyone in the family.

We do not believe that any woman was ever liberated by a thin patty of beef smothered with a large variety of condiments and served on a bun which tastes like a paper plate and does little more than hold the hamburger in place. No woman ever recovered from overwork by listlessly consuming a greasy bagful of french fries. No woman ever put variety back in her life by spooning down a zillion calorie thick shake. All she did was consume a lot of extra calories, a lot of extra fat, a lot of extra sugar to divert her body from burning up the stored fat she already had. All she did was give in to overtaste.

If the only break you got today was a lightning trip to a fast food chain, then you are in big trouble, lady, and you had better watch yourself.

The worst thing about a homemaker's life is not that it is hard to do all the work, but that the constant repetition is difficult and boring.

If you had one of those paying jobs in factories where workers do the same thing over and over and over again, the boss would go out and hire an industrial psychologist with all kinds of advanced degrees to keep you from getting bored and irritable. This genius would make the boss spend great fortunes to pipe interesting music into the factory, paint the walls in compatible colors, and circulate you through the process so you would not have to do the same job forever, but could switch from one job to another.

Today, universities offer courses are on how to keep up the morale of the bored assembly line worker and how to keep productivity soaring.

If the morale and productivity of the factory worker fall, the national economy suffers. If your morale and your productivity fall, then your pleasure economy and that of your whole family suffers.

Consequently, we worry about the woman whose life has resolved itself into a pattern—a holding pattern. We know the most difficult thing for her to arrange is a change in her pattern.

Many women may not recognize at first that the household life involves a serious pleasure deficit. Nevertheless, they may never feel miserable, lonesome or put-down. They may never utter a word of complaint.

The wonderful and reliable pleasures that come with marriage—sexual fulfillment, the happiness of parenthood, companionship, sharing, emotional security—may all be in proper working order. In fact, the only way to tell that many young housewives are compensating for some unknown pleasure deficit through excess taste gratification is to observe that slowly—very, very slowly—they are gaining weight.

Marie H. was married at the young age of eighteen, and became pregnant almost immediately. She was a slim, pretty girl. Her husband was in the Navy and while she was pregnant, he went on a tour of duty in the Pacific area. "It all started after I was married," she wrote. "When I was pregnant in my fifth month, I could not stop myself from eating candy. After my pregnancy, I was ten pounds overweight. Two months later, not realizing I was so overweight, I went shopping for a size fourteen dress and I came home with the only one that would fit me at my 174 pounds—a size 18½!"

In June 1971, Marie began dieting according to the guidelines for sensible eating set forth in the Long Beach Diet that was included with the over-the-counter product she was using to help her control her appetite. As a result, she lost almost 50 pounds!

"Candy medication for weight control has helped me all the way. When I get hungry, I take a candy medication and a glass of water, and follow the instructions in the little booklet. I owe my success to that candy medication."

As Marie's child grows older, as her married life becomes more fluid and less confining, she will find new pleasures to substitute for overtasting.

Until that time comes, she is re-training her sense of taste toward enjoyment of less fattening foods and thereby exercising a newfound control of her appetite. And when that time comes, she will have developed a new sense of taste and a workable, lifelong system of dieting without suffering.

One woman we spoke to complained that the reason she had become overweight was that "a lot of the time, we have not had enough money to buy the proper foods to reduce on."

The point she made was familiar to us; we recognized this problem.

Some of our patients are the children of people who have had prolonged job troubles, who have had to seek public relief from time to time. Some of our patients have mothers who are alone and have to support the family single-handed. Others come from homes where every penny counts and there just is not any extra money. This applies to more and more homes these days. A mother may know perfectly well that pasta and potatoes and high fat content meats like hot dogs and pork chops will make her fat, but she has got to stretch the food dollar, and those items are supposed to be among "dollar stretchers."

The former governor of a great state once got into a fight with a welfare mother who was leading a demonstration. His accusation was that she did not have anything to complain about since she was so big and fat. What that governor did not understand was that the welfare mother was fat because she had spent her life eating bread, sugar, beans, rice, and packaged cake. He thought that her fat indicated that she was living well, when what it really meant was that she was eating badly. The poor eat poorly.

Women in their markets and their kitchens know their food dollar intimately. They know just how far it will go, and very often they try to stretch it at their own expense. They buy enough meat for their children and their husband, but not enough for themselves. They make enough salad for their children and their husbands but not enough for themselves. We know a woman who grew up in a low-income home in Brooklyn who recalled, "I was always looking in the pot, to see if my mother had left herself a piece of chicken."

We are well aware that many mothers today do not leave themselves much nutritional food at all. They feed themselves the second-class foods, short-changing their own nutrition.

One terrible syndrome we see all the time has nothing to do with poverty, but concerns the psychology of women who put themselves at the short end of their food dollar.

The children come home from school for a lunch of

soup, a sandwich and a piece of pie. They eat most of the meal leaving the crusts of bread and pie. Then, they return to school. Instead of throwing away the leftovers, or digging them into a garden pot for compost, the mother eats them. That is her lunch.

All this is done while she is on her feet, clearing the table, without thinking about it. In fact, if somebody asked her whether she had lunch today, she would not remember whether she did or not because the process of eating leftovers is so casual and hurried, that it leaves no taste impression.

This is what we mean when we say "overtasting" is really "undertasting." We advise our mothers to feed themselves according to our Rules for Enlightened Feeding. In addition, we advise them to sit down and eat slowly. They are shortchanging their own nutrition by cooking good food for everyone else in the family to the exclusion of themselves. These are the habits that make slim young wives into fat young mothers.

As for money, it simply does not have to cost a fortune to eat sensibly if you know what you are doing. It is just as inexpensive to have a side dish of pasta with a main course salad as it is to have a main course of pasta with salad on the side. It is just as cheap to eat tuna fish on whole wheat crackers as it is to eat it on what we call "gum wad" bread.

Try another experiment: Take a slice of bread out of the loaf you ordinarily buy in the supermarket and squeeze it in the palm of your hand. If it crumbles, you probably bought the kind of bread we like to see our patients eat. If it squashes into a mass resembling a wad of gum, it is the type of bread we wish to leave eliminated from the diet of everyone.

The price of meat is going to be high whether the meat has fat or not. So cut off the fat, and cut down on meat—use chicken or fish, instead. It is good nutritional practice and cheaper to broil meat than to fry. Save some money, and the potential for heart trouble by broiling.

When Mrs. E. was first married, she thought she was overweight at 135 pounds. She had ambitions for her body: she wanted to be beautiful. But as she allowed her life to become a humdrum routine in the holding pattern of homemaking, her image of herself began to change. Her pressure to stay beautiful lessened. She thought that nobody cared if you are fifteen pounds overweight, you have to be really fat to get the attention of society. Mrs. E. had stopped giving herself enough of her own attention and she had stopped caring herself. Nobody else was distressed if she carried a little extra weight. Because she was not distressed she continued to gain without noticing.

This subtle, slow process went on for years. In fact, by the time she had been married for about fifteen years, Mrs. E. weighed 225 pounds. It alarmed her family.

However, they did not do anything to help her lose weight. They would continue to "love" her no matter how big she was, and therefore, they did not consider her diet important enough to allow her to alter their eating habits while she altered hers. (We put "love" in quotation marks because we do not think that is love. Remember, the opposite of love is not hate, but rather, not caring.) If her family had really loved her, they would have spoken up sooner.

Eventually, those children who had been tying Mrs. E. down to the house all those years, giving her some pleasures but preventing her from enjoying others, grew up and left home. They got married and found their own lives, leaving Mrs. E. with an empty nest.

She was now alone with her husband, and her main reminder of all her years of motherhood was 100 pounds of extra weight. She had not worked since her marriage and she now had absolutely nothing to do. Throughout the best years of her life she had been fat and when she became a grandmother, no one cared at all whether she was shapely or not.

What happened? She had a gigantic pleasure deficit which required her to get more taste pleasure economy now than ever before!

For this woman to go on a diet at this stage of life is an enormous endeavor. To whom can she turn? What assistance can she get? She is used to eating huge quantities of food. How can she possibly learn to get the same taste pleasure from less food?

Nevertheless, Mrs. E. set out in January 1972 to lose at least fifty pounds. She had decided that she was going to try to recapture her original pre-marital figure. To control her rampant desire to overtaste, she needed an extra boost.

As she wrote, "I have found that chewing gum medication for weight control keeps me from being hungry. At least it keeps my jaws going. I am lonesome a lot, I need to talk to people, and maybe keeping my jaws going gives me the feeling that I am talking. . . ."

By the end of 1972, Mrs. E. had lost her fifty pounds. She felt better and she looked better. Maybe she will never be 135 pounds again, but at least she regained her old image of herself—the image of a woman with a reason to look good.

Mrs. M. began to put on weight after the birth of her first child. She is five feet seven inches tall, and believed that her ideal weight was 145 pounds. That is what she

149

weighed in high school when she established her most appealing self-image.

In June 1970, she weighed 233 pounds. But somehow, with the habitual blindness of one who looked at herself every day, but not too carefully, she did not realize the extent of the damage.

"One day," she wrote, "I was over at my mother's house. There were quite a few people there. One man whom I had not seen for some time came up to me and said, 'Louise, what the hell are you doing to yourself? You've put on quite a few pounds!' "

It was a slap in the face to her, but it made a positive impression.

"From that moment on," Mrs. M. wrote, "I was determined to lose weight. I enrolled in a figure salon. I went through belts and bikes and exercises three times a week for about two or three hours each time. I did lose weight in a few weeks, but the results were going too slow for me."

It had taken her a couple of years to get really fat, and now she wanted to reverse that process in just a couple of weeks.

Overtasting has, for one reason or another, become one of our greatest pleasures in life, and it is not going to be easy to give up quickly. A few pounds in a few weeks is a perfectly sound and reasonable rate of weight loss in any diet. You did not increase your size quickly and you cannot expect to decrease your size quickly.

"I could not get my mind off food," Mrs. M. related. "Then I would chew medicated gum for weight control and that would refresh me. It was sort of strange. One minute I was tense and nervous because I was trying to keep away from food (and that can work very much on a person, especially when you are trying to lose weight so badly). Then I took one or two pieces of gum medication and I would feel as though I had just finished an ice cream sundae or a strawberry shortcake."

Here, then, was a clear indication to us that it was the taste of sweetness, not all the fattening, rich, creamy desserts that carry the taste, that was satisfying Mrs. M. Using the slow, more sure method of appetite control through taste control, Mrs. M. lost over 60 pounds!

Mrs. S. of Minnesota is a tall, athletic woman with four children. At five feet nine inches tall, she had always been a tall "skinny kid" and she rather liked herself that way. While carrying her last baby, she gained 23 pounds. "I came out of the hospital weighing 159 pounds," she stated. "That is too fat for me."

When she announced to her husband that she was overweight, he began bringing diets home to her from his gym. However, Mrs. S. was home for the fourth time with an infant, and she just could not stop eating.

"I tried every freak diet that came along," she said. The first of these was starvation. "Normally, I have an atrocious appetite and get crabby and sick when I do not eat." To avoid becoming so upset she tried something else besides starvation.

Her next diet attempt was a "water diet." "I lost eight pounds in two weeks and put it all back the minute I started eating normally again."

After that, she tried the grapefruit diet which resulted in acid indigestion and then the chicken diet which brought on boredom.

Finally, she decided to try the recommended rules for sensible eating she found in a package of candy medication for weight control. Those maddening fifteen pounds, which she had been trying to lose for over six months, finally came off—and stayed off. She is back in her usual size clothes now. The baby boy is now a toddler and she gets some exercise with him. After her experience, she is now very careful. "I keep candy weight control medication in the cupboard all the time, just in case."

We do not want you to give up eating nor do we want you to give up tasting. We only want you to get through these crucial years without getting fat, when you are a young mother with enormous tasks and responsibilities. When the children leave home for school, we want you to be able to enjoy your new found free time.

If you can control your sense of taste during these crucial, wonderful, but difficult years, you will make your life more wonderful and less difficult.

CHAPTER 7

"Chronic Pleasure Need" and the Ailing Dieter

There are some physical and emotional situations which put so much pain continually into a person's life that they are literally forever trying to compensate themselves with sensual pleasure through overtaste. We call this person the "compulsive eater."

When stress arises from tensions in life, in love, the compulsive eater eats! The damage she does is twofold: she is not actually facing and trying to cope with his stress situation; and, he is damaging his body by overeating. If you allow a hunger pain to take first place in your concern it will mask the true pain in your heart, the insult to your vanity, or the pain of rejection of your work or your love. If you oversatisfy your taste needs, you ignore the demands life has placed upon you. When this becomes a fixed, habitual way of handling conflicts, we call this a "chronic pleasure need."

It may calm down, but it never really goes away. Chronic pleasure need affects thousands of people who have some miserable emotional or physical situation affecting their lives through outside circumstances. They are in constant search of some extra pleasure to make life more bearable. For such people dieting is sometimes so difficult that psychiatric help is needed.

In examining letters from people who had written of their experiences, we were impressed by the number of people who suffered from various ailments that interfered with their ability to follow a healthy, prudent diet. These people indicated how, using candy medication for weight control, they were able to curb the need for snacks and sweets that was contributing to their weight problem. The treatment and prevention of obesity, can make the difference between handling a health problem in a direct and productive way, or losing sight of it under a virtual blanket of fat.

"I used gum weight control medication to help me control my overeating," wrote Mrs. R. "I wanted to gain control over my childhood conditioning. 'Essen! Essen! Eat! Eat!'" I was told. "'Do not waste food!' It numbed my taste buds, which I was happy about. I did not want to want food at that time."

Here was the explanation. She wrote of her youth, her ambitions, and of the many things on her mind. She had figured out that overeating occurred with her at times of psychological stress. Since her overweight was compounding the stress, she was smart enough to decide upon eliminating the sensual compensatory overtasting in favor of the pleasure of becoming slim again. She reduced from size eighteen down to a size eight!

"I cannot say that the gum medication for weight control killed my appetite; I still wanted to eat. But, I found that after eating a certain amount I could be satisfied if I used the gum instead of another portion of food!"

To end Mrs. R's story, we would like to include this item to show the strength of habits and attractions of a lifetime. Recently, she recalled, after entertaining her family at dinner and knowing that she had eaten enough, something happened that she never expected. Her brother had brought fresh bagels which she had avoided at the table. As she was putting the leftovers away, she picked up the bagels with the memory of her family fresh in her mind, and was overcome with a desire to eat them. "All of my common sense was telling me, 'Don't do it! Don't do it! But you know what? I could not resist, I had to take a bite out of a bagel! But that is all I took, one bite! Then I very quickly wrapped the rest and put them away."

That bagel suddenly appeared as the symbol of life before growing up, before tension, before anxiety, before pain. We all have our "bagels," our symbols of fun and the good old days. The proof of Mrs. R's victory over "compensatory overtaste" was the one bite missing from the bagels she put away that night.

CHAPTER 8

You Need All the Taste You Can Get!

We never intended to extend the Ages of Overtaste into the age range of the so-called senior citizen. But we received a letter from one gentleman whose story was so exhilarating that we feel compelled to offer it, as a simple guide for those who are getting older, but do not wish to get fatter.

Quentin B., a Canadian, had always been a vigorous and athletic man, full of life, and schemes and pleasures. One day when he was in his seventies, he went to his doctor for a checkup and was told by his doctor that those pleasures were "getting a little out of hand." It is always a tremendous shock to be told that you must give up the delights of a lifetime, especially if you had delights like Quentin.

"I have been overweight for the past fifteen years," he wrote. "I have had a ravenous craving for hearty meals for a lifetime.... My best meal was always an early breakfast: meat, potatoes, bread and butter, coffee, milk and sugar, to wind up with a quarter of a pie, jam or marmalade. I also relish all sorts of fish, vegetables, salads, and an apple or two daily. I never decline a substantial main dish of deer steak, roast of moose, cabbage, browned potatoes with roast wild hare, likewise partridge, duck, wild goose and chicken or turkey; onions with all meats are great with me, raw, fried or boiled...."

156

Deer, moose, hare, and geese, sound more like Paul Bunyan's menu than the eating habits of an ordinary human being! But as a matter of fact, Mr. B. is from the great Canadian outdoors, whose eating habits were established many years ago before there was a trailer park or an American gas company in Canada. For him, deer, moose, hare and geese are run-of-the-mill dishes; and he loved every morsel of them for nearly seventy-five years.

"I have never indulged in any intoxicating drinks," Mr. B. confided. "I have smoked non-filtered cigarettes for the last fifty-eight years. . . . I seldom go to bed before midnight, and am up and rested at 6 A.M. daily."

Furthermore, he builds up his body so that it can take the beating he gives it when he sits down to eat. "I have been a good swimmer, a baseball and hockey player, and an ardent snowshoer. Back in the twenties, I won an award for a 198 mile shoe tramp in a total of 52 hours and 15 minutes . . . I take a good one-hour walk each day."

Other than his own personal attitudes, perhaps the secret of Mr. B's explosive enjoyment of life was the fact that he was a teacher most of his life, always surrounded by young people. How often have we pediatricians been known to say: "My children keep me young"?

However, all the good hard living began to have an adverse effect on him. At the age of seventy-five, he weighed 240 pounds, about 75 pounds more than he should have. But just because you are strong does not mean you are not overweight when you are 240 pounds. All of a sudden, the doctor said there was a strain on his heart. Even this seemingly healthy man, who had never been sick in his life, was beginning to weaken under the load of his own body.

Mr. B. did not need any special psychological stimulation to get him started on a diet. He had quite enough drive to do anything he decided to do. "I am a born optimist," he wrote. "Cheerful, active and enjoying life to its fullest measure. A weakness . . . well, I do love the ladies. . . ."

"I tried gum medication for weight control," reported Mr. B., "and the result was that my appetite was controlled, weight recorded on scale down to 168 pounds. I truthfully owe it all to gum medication." Mr. B. was perhaps over-generous but gum weight control medication can help in the transitional process of re-training overtaste buds. "In summary, I am feeling 100 percent better and lady friends congratulate me for looking much younger."

It seems clear that as our taste buds and our bodies grow older appetite naturally decreases, and you may not have to diet at all. In fact, if we were in the practice of caring for the elderly, and one of our patients started dieting strenuously, we would probably discourage him.

We do ask you to remember, whatever Age of Overtaste you are involved with, that the key to appetite control is taste control. If you are a mother whose middle-aged children are overweight, keep reminding them that they may have the bad tasting habits you unwittingly gave them when you were a young parent, and put them, on their present taste control.

If you have health problems that your physician relates to bad eating habits, try to let your experience work for the good of your offspring. Do not be a candy-dispensing grandparent. Try to help your children raise, your grandchildren with the proper eating habits.

We believe that if we all work together, we can raise a new, healthier generation of people, just by learning that dieting, like every lifestyle, is a matter of taste.

CHAPTER 9

How To Eat Well, Get Slim and Stay Slim: 10 Guidelines

I. *Dieting means eating* ("diet—1. to cause to take food; 2. to cause to eat and drink according to prescribed rules" —Webster's *Third New International Dictionary*). Dieting does *not* mean deprivation; it means moderation.

II. *Sensible eating is positive dieting.* Learn the nutritional principles that should govern your daily eating. Once you put them into practice, *you are already on a weight control diet* (and so is the rest of your family).

III. *The only good diet is a pleasurable one.* If you don't enjoy your daily diet, or it does not include food that pleases your sense of taste, you will never succeed in making it a lifetime pattern—and sooner or later you will drift back into your old bad habits.

IV. *The key to weight control is taste control.* Once you learn the difference between a pang of real hunger and the craving for a pleasurable taste, you will find yourself eating less and enjoying it more.

V. *Don't start a diet when you are troubled by other serious worries or pressures*—you have enough tension to deal with as it is.

VI. *Don't diet in secret*—let everyone know you are determined to control your weight. But remember no one can be with you all the time watching what you eat.

VII. *Never reward children with desserts, sodas, cookies or candy,* and never punish them by withholding desserts or other special-treat foods. Educate your child's sense of taste so that sweets are no longer seductive.

VIII. *Practice what you preach.* Children will not learn the right lessons unless their parents' good eating habits are usually seen and not heard.

IX. *One ounce of prevention is worth ten pounds of cure.* Preventing one ounce of fat cells from developing in childhood may stave off ten pounds of fat in an overweight adult.

X. *If food is love, then your love for your children should be measured not by how much you feed them but how wisely.*

BE CONFIDENT. BE PATIENT. BE RESOLUTE—AND *YOU WILL SUCCEED.* (AND SO WILL YOUR FAMILY.)

CHAPTER 10

Combat Tips for Fighting "the Battle of the Bulge"

Anthony A. Conte, M.D., a colleague of ours and a bariatrician (weight control specialist) from Beaver, Pennsylvania, hands his patients this list of Combat tips.

1. *Eat Slower.* It sounds simple, but the longer you take to eat, the less hungry you'll feel between· meals. It's often helpful to use a smaller plate as well, to make portions appear larger. Savor every bite, enjoy every mouthful of food like it was your last. You'll be surprised how satisfied you'll feel.
2. *Weigh Yourself Only Once A Week At the Same Time.* If you are losing weight, you will know it soon enough by the way your clothes fit. There is no need to measure each ounce lost—it's better to wait for the pounds to fall.
3. *Don't Eat Standing Up.* Make it a rule to make very meal an event. Eat sitting down. Don't stand in front of the refrigerator "tasting" foods while deciding what to eat. You'll aid digestion if you're totally relaxed and comfortable at mealtimes.
4. *Resist Temptation.* It is easier said than done, but try at any cost to resist the temptation to eat that extra portion or between-meal snack. To help resist overeating, curb your appetite with a tasty, medicated candy.

5. *Drink Plenty Of Water.* At least 8 full glasses of water a day is especially beneficial while dieting. Not only is it good for you, but it will help maintain a feeling of fullness all day long.

6. *Keep Busy.* Staying active and busy is another good way to divert your attention from food. Instead of snacking in front of the television, go to a movie, or develop a hobby. The busier you are, the less time you'll have to think about eating.

7. *Follow the meat/fish rule.* Concentrate on eating less fattening meats. Beef and lamb often contain large amounts of fat. The more fish, poultry and veal you eat, the better your chances of losing weight.

8. *Avoid High Calorie Foods.* Baked goods, chocolate, soft cheese and canned fruits are all high calorie foods to be avoided. Concentrate on a regimen of good, fresh, high protein, nutritionally balanced food. If you must satisfy a sweet tooth, the appetite-curbing, low calorie candies may help.

9. *Reduce Drinking.* A dieter is wise to avoid alcoholic beverages, some of which are as high in calories as an ice cream soda. White wine is the lowest calorie alcoholic beverage, and may even be helpful in curbing that sweet tooth during the evening hours.

10. *Think About The New You.* One of the best ways to stay on a diet is to think about how much better you'll look and feel once those pounds are gone. Think about the compliments you'll receive and how much more attractive you will be to others.

11. *Stay In Bed.* Those midnight raids on the ice box are a shortcut to obesity. When hunger strikes, drink some water, read a book, or wake up your spouse. By all means, try to stay in bed. And of course, reducing the amount of dietary cheating you can do in the middle of the night.

12. *Don't Be Discouraged—Don't Be A Quitter.* Many people experience greatest weight loss the first week, less during the second week. Don't lose faith—the safest way to slim down is to lose weight the same way it was gained—one pound at a time.

Cheating On Your Diet Is Like Cheating On Yourself

Many of our patients ask, "Doctor, I just don't understand why Mrs. Brown lost almost three pounds last week, but I didn't lose an ounce. We're both following the Long Beach 14-Day Diet you recommend. Do I have some special problem?"

We answer this commonly asked question with some simple arithmetic. The average overweight patient consumes approximately 2400 calories a day. When our patients follow the Long Beach Diet we prescribe, they consume about 1200-1400 calories per day. That means that while the patient is dieting, she's operating with a 1200 calorie deficit per day. Multiplied by seven days in a week the patient now consumes 8400 calories *less* per week.

It takes 3500 calories less to eliminate a pound of fat. Now divide 8400 calories by the 3500 calories in a pound and you'll get 2.7 pounds of body fat which is about how much you should lose during the first week of the Long Beach Diet.

If you don't lose weight on the Long Beach Diet, your special problem is you. You're a dietary cheat. We guarantee you won't lose a pound if you don't mend your sinful ways, and that you could lose approximately 2.7 pounds if you diet prudently.

The Fast Food "Baddies"

With the merry-go-round that most American seem
to ride most of the time, fast foods have become almost
a way of life. Sure these foods are fast, but they are
loaded with calories. Few people will stop and think how
many calories are in that lunch at the local hamburger
counter. The great American lunch—a hamburger,
french fries and a shake—could cost you as much as
1200 calories, depending on how "glorified" the burger
is. That is just about as many calories as a dieter should
eat in a whole day. This chart listing the calorie value of
leading fast food places should be of interest to you.
After reading this, we are sure you will spend a little
extra time to prepare your own meals.

Calorie Chart

Arby's
Junior Roast Beef 240
Roast Beef 429
Turkey Sandwich with dressing . . 402
  (without Arby's dressing) 337
Super Roast Beef. 705

Arthur Treacher's Fish & Chips
Fish, Chips and coleslaw:
  3-piece dinner 1100
  2-piece dinner 905

Baskin Robbins
One scoop with sugar cone:
  Chocolate Fudge 229
  French Vanilla 217
  Rocky Road 204
  Butter Pecan 195
  Chocolate Mint 189
  Jamoca 182
  Fresh Strawberry 168
  Fresh Peach 165
  Mango Sherbet 132
  Banana Daiquiri Ice 129

Bridgeman's
Vanilla Ice Cream (plain cone) . . . 170
Vanilla Ice Cream (sugar cone) . . 200

("Calorie content does not increase appreciably for other flavors," a Bridgeman's spokesman said.)

Burger Chef
Hamburger 250
Double Hamburger 325
Super Chef 530
Big Chef 535
French Fries 240
Chocolate Shake 310

Burger King
Whopper 630
Whopper Junior 285
Double Hamburger 325
Hamburger 252
Cheeseburger 305
Hot Dog. 291
Whaler 744
French Fries 220
Chocolate Shake 365

Chicken Delight
½ Chicken (4 pieces) 625

Colonel Sanders
15-piece Bucket. 3300
One Drumstick 220
3-piece Special 660
Dinner (Chicken, mashed potatoes, gravy, coleslaw, roll),
  2-piece Original 595
  2-piece Crispy 665
  3-piece Original 830
  3-piece Crispy 1070

Dairy Queen
Small Cone 110
Medium Cone. 230
Large Cone. 340
Small Dipped Cone 160
Medium Dipped Cone 310
Large Dipped Cone 450
Small Sundae. 190
Medium Sundae 300
Large Sundae 430
Small Malt 400
Medium Malt 580
Large Malt 800
Hot Fudge Brownie Delight
  Sundae 580

Banana Split 580	Fish Sandwich.................275
Parfait 460	Hot Dog.......................265
Dilly Bar 240	French Fries 155
DQ Sandwich.................190	Milk Shake (8 oz.) 320
Buster Bar 390	Apple Turnover...............290
Super Brazier 850	

Howard Johnson's

Brazier Cheeseburger 310	Small Cone, Vanilla 186
Big Brazier Deluxe 540	Chocolate....................195
Big Brazier...................510	Medium, Cone, Vanilla 247
Brazier Dog 270	Chocolate....................261
Super Brazier Dog 500	Large Cone, Vanilla 370
Brazier Chili Dog..............330	Chocolate....................390
Brazier 250	Sherbet.......................136
Brazier Barbecue 280	7-oz. pkg. Fried Clams 357
Bos'n's Mate Fish Sandwich 340	1/8 of Pecan Pie 474
Chicken Pack..................342	
French Fries 200	**McDonald's**
Onion Rings 300	Egg McMuffin 312

(Dipped Cones, Sundaes, Malts/
Shakes calorie listings are all for
chocolate flavor.)

Hotcakes, Sausage, Syrup.......507
Dunkin' Donuts	Hamburger 249
Plain Cake Donut..............240	Double Hamburger............350
Plain Honey Dipped 260	Cheeseburger 309
Plain (White Icing) 265	Quarter Pounder...............414
Plain (Chocolate Icing)........235	Quarter Pounder w/Cheese 521
Chocolate Cake 240	Big Mac 557
Chocolate Honey Dipped.......250	Filet-O-Fish 406
Yeast-Raised Donuts (Jelly, Custard,	French Fries 215
or Cream fillings):	Hot Apple Pie..................265
Sugared 255	Chocolate Shake 317
Honey Dipped 275	Vanilla Shake 322
(Add 50 calories for fillings)	Strawberry Shake 315
Plain Coffee Roll with Glaze......250	**Pizza Hut**
Sugared Bismarck 245	Cheese Pizza:
Bismarck with White Icing 270	Individual—Thick Crust 1030
Butternut Donut 220	Thin Crust 1005
	½ of 13-inch Thick Crust 900
Hardee's	Thin Crust 850
Huskie Deluxe 525	½ of 15-inch Thick Crust 1200
Huskie Junior.................475	Thin Crust 1150
	Red Barn
	Cheese Buster 707

French Fries 108

Shake 358

Salad 189

Apple Pie 217

Taco Bell

Enchirito 391

Frijole 231

White Castle

Hamburger 164

Cheeseburger 198

Fish Sandwich............... 200

French Fries 219

Onion Rings 341

Milk Shake................... 213

Cinnamon Roll 305

Cherry Roll.................. 334

Zantigo

Taco 146

Tostada 206

Burrito 345

Reprinted with permission from *Minneapolis Tribune.*

Conclusion

You've read the book . . . now write your own success story. *Bon Appétit!*